It's A Love Thing:
Leading with Heart to Transform Schools

William H. Parker

Copyright © 2025 by William H. Parker.

All Rights Reserved. This book, nor any portion thereof, may be reproduced or used in any manner whatsoever without the expressed written permission of the author except for the use of brief quotations in a book review.

ISBN: 979-8-9993193-2-6

Printed in the United States of America.

Edited, Formatted and Published by Empower Her Publishing, LLC

empowerherpublishing.com

Dedication

This book is dedicated to my wife, Pamela, and my sons, Justin and Billy, who encouraged me to write a book highlighting some of the valuable and vital lessons learned during my school leadership journey.

I have been extremely fortunate and blessed in my career to work with extraordinary people who showed me the power of placing love and compassion at the center of our work. They taught me that leading with heart, courage, and care in the classroom, school, and school district can transform lives and drive outstanding student achievement.

To the school leaders who read this book, I hope you gain practical insights that help you elevate your impact with students and staff, foster positive change in your school, and achieve exceptional student success.

Table of Contents

Chapter 1: *Instructional Leadership at its Core*..................…...3

Chapter 2: *School Vision*...15

Chapter 3: *Creating a Community of Caring*........................25

Chapter 4: *Building Relationships*...................................47

Chapter 5: *Teamwork: We are Better Together*......................55

Chapter 6: *Distributive Leadership: Lead with Me*...................63

Chapter 7: *The Power of Instructional Delivery*......................73

Chapter 8: *The Use of Data in Decision Making*....................105

Chapter 9: *Care Enough to Confront*..................…..............121

Chapter 10: *Champions Are Made in the Off-Season*...............131

Chapter 11: *Message to New Principals*.............................141

Foreword

Bill Parker just hit the ball out of the park with *It's A Love Thing*! Three elements of this book stick like new glue. First is the 'practicality' of this work; you can use all or parts of the book immediately and it will make a significant difference in your instructional efforts. Leading with love will always send you in the right direction. Second, the 'power' of this huge message is exactly the key to leveraging collaborative synergy in schools. Finally, the 'precise' advice and direction interwoven into real life examples provide readers with clear leadership examples to follow.

Mr. Parker provides vibrant models of the culture and coherence that successful leaders have developed and demonstrated to lift students, teachers, parents, and the community. Understanding the importance of kindness, knowing students' names, affirming teachers and students alike, and having a deep, deep conviction about every child, every day is directly tied to academic and personal success. Details of true instructional leaders turbo-charging students are illuminated throughout each page. Building capacity, using data, loving learning and loving each other will always work.

Mr. Parker is one of the finest and most important leaders I have worked with. I have learned a lot from him, and can confidently confirm that teacher leaders, principals and central office leaders will find tremendous value and motivation within this book. They will clearly understand that indeed, *It's A Love Thing*.

Dr. Mark Edwards
2013 AASA Superintendent of the Year
Author & Leadership Consultant

Dr. Mark Edwards served as a school superintendent for 25 years and is widely recognized as a leader in digital innovation. He has published four books: *Every Child, Every Day*, *Thank You for Your Leadership*, and, most recently, he co-authored *Unstoppable Momentum* and *Spirit Work and the Science of Collaboration* with Michael Fullan.

In 2013, Dr. Edwards was named the AASA National Superintendent of the Year as well as the North Carolina Superintendent of the Year. He served as Superintendent of the Mooresville Graded School District for nine years, leading the district to national and international acclaim as a model of excellence. Prior to that, he was Superintendent of Henrico County, Virginia for ten years, and in 2001, he was named Virginia Superintendent of the Year. In 2000, he led the first district-wide one-to-one laptop program in the nation.

Over the course of his career, Dr. Edwards has received numerous awards, including the Harold W. McGraw, Jr. Prize in Education, the *eSchool News* Tech-Savvy Superintendent Award, Common Sense Media's National Educator of the Year, and National Educator honors from the Academy of Arts and Sciences. In 2017, he was recognized as one of the Top Thirty Transformational Leaders by the Center for Digital Learning. His leadership has been acknowledged by President Barack Obama, Governor Jeb Bush, Governor Bob Wise, Governor Jim Hunt, and Senator Mark Warner.

Beyond his work in K–12 education, Dr. Edwards has also served as Dean of the College of Education at the University of North Alabama, Senior Vice President of Discovery Education, and CEO of Challenge U. He and his wife have been married for 41 years and are the proud parents of three children.

It's A Love Thing:
Leading with Heart to Transform Schools

William H. Parker

"Sometimes it takes only one act of kindness and caring to change a person's life."
—Jackie Chan

Chapter 1
Instructional Leadership at its Core

Instructional leadership is demanding and challenging work, but it is also exciting, fulfilling and gratifying when a school community collaborates and achieves at its highest levels. To initiate effective learning in an environment of safety, order and high expectations, the cornerstone of this noble work must be love — a high regard and value for people. When striving to accomplish exceptional success in a school community, love should be deeply rooted within the school's culture, its mission and vision, and any relationship with collaborative partnerships. Love should be clearly reflected in the school's use of data and in the monitoring of student progress. It should be evident in the delivery of instruction and clear in the importance of professional growth and building of leadership capacity.

Leadership, by any stretch of the imagination, is difficult; however, instructional leadership is more than a notion, more than a mere position, more than being in charge. So before endeavoring to take on such a role, consider the following questions:

- Why seek an instructional leadership position that requires managing curriculum and instruction? One that demands leading a school community of students, teachers, staff, and parents?
- What drives you to serve and support students, teachers, parents, and colleagues and do so with uniqueness?
- Do you seek such a role for the position, the perks, the pay, the privileges, or the power?

- Are you inspired, motivated, and committed to making a difference in your school community's performance and success?

Though thought-provoking, the questions are more about the technical aspects of instructional leadership. Through education and experience, the nod to yes seems more likely and the questions more easily answered. Leadership, in general, is a two-sided coin and instructional leadership is no different. The following questions get at the heart of the matter: *How deep is your love for your school community? Where is your heart when it comes to caring about and serving others?* Instructional leadership, from my perspective, is a "love thing." One must lead with love! From decades of experience in my career as a teacher, department chair, assistant principal, principal and central office executive, I have witnessed the powerful difference that love, compassion, and deeply valuing a school community can make in the education system. Instructional leadership, then, is more than the knowledge of pedagogy. While understanding the art and science of teaching and learning is essential for instructional leadership, the other side of the coin is compassion – love. It is about caring passionately, intently and vigorously enough to create the positive change in the school community which elevates achievement. Success in a school community doesn't just happen. It takes impassioned and committed instructional leaders to chart the course and create the school culture and climate which facilitate such success.

Love is the greatest force in the universe, and it continues to impact the institutions of marriage, family, religion, education, government, the economy, and healthcare. When love is demonstrated, it motivates us to take increased action to make our school community, and the world, a better place to serve and uplift people. As Albert Ellis once stated, "The art of love is largely the art of persistence." Love, then, is an action. With this premise, how school leadership conducts business with intentionality, determination, and persistence are critical to guiding and directing school communities to exceptional success. Love must be the driving force behind decisions and actions that advance the school community. It must also be at the core of the school's mission as those charged with carrying out the mission minister to students and teams. Love empowers those in leadership positions to be bold, resolute, and determined.

Reflecting personally upon the teachers, coaches and administrators who influenced and impacted my life, I realize they were individuals who wholeheartedly poured their love and support into me. They understood that love cultivates, prepares and lifts. They lived out the words of the Dalai Lama, "the prime purpose in life is to help others." These educators put their love in action. They made certain I did my work to meet or exceed standards. They managed and led the classroom well to ensure there was a respectful, caring environment, conducive for learning. They provided additional time and instruction when I struggled or had difficulty grasping certain material. They explained assignments and content clearly, fully, and in a variety of ways to ensure that I understood it. They took the necessary time to get to know me as an individual, to understand my background, my circumstances, and my uniqueness. They exhibited what Elbert Hubbard once said, "A friend is someone who knows all about you and still loves you." I am positive proof and a testament to how their love can lift a student. From timidity and doubt to achievement and confidence, love is a crucial ingredient in lifting students to extraordinary success levels. Love lifted me! Even me!

"Love recognizes no barriers. It jumps hurdles, leaps fences, penetrates walls to arrive at its destination full of hope." — Maya Angelou

Love is at the core of our just cause as school leaders and is a key motivator for increasing student performances. In a caring and compassionate setting, every child matters. I Repeat! Every Child Matters! Remember that everything we do sends a message about who we are and about whom we value. Love is the catalyst to elevating every child every day, not just some of the children some of the time. Not focusing on every child is troubling and damaging. Love must motivate every educator to rise up in the morning with conviction, commitment, and courage to ensure he or she is meeting the needs of every child, every day.

Dr. Cleo Davis was one of my teachers and coaches at Ballou Senior High School in SE Washington, DC, from 1969-1971. If you know anything about DC, southeast is probably the toughest part of the city. Other than my mother and father, Cleo had the biggest impact on my life. He was that educator! I credit my desire and interest to work with young people in education due to his example and influence. I'm sure you can stroll down your own "memory lane" and identify a special teacher who inspired you to pursue a career in education and who also guided other young people toward excellence. I know you stand on their shoulders as I stand on the shoulders of Dr. Cleo Davis.

In June 2016, I had the great honor of speaking at Cleo's 75th birthday party and shared how his love changed my trajectory in life. In the mid to late 1960s, I was a rascal — restless and rebellious, a real piece of work, stubborn as hell. For anyone outside of my family, I was hard to love. Have you ever, perhaps, encountered similar students? Cleo could have taken the position of apathy, indifference and not given a damn. Or he could have ignored me or taken the posture of "why bother?" He had every reason to keep me at a distance and to overlook or ignore me. I suppose he saw some "gleaming and redeeming" qualities in me, so he took a chance on a poor boy and committed the effort and energy to make a difference. As a result, my life changed, and I began to move in a more positive direction. Cleo understood what Hubert H. Humphrey meant when he said, "The greatest healing therapy is love."

I know you remember the old gospel song, "Love Lifted Me." The hymn refers to a person who was lost and sinking, living on the margins, and then was amazingly redeemed, reclaimed, and restored to a place of worth and victory because of "love." Reaching out with compassion can turn a life around. When instructional leaders are ambassadors of love, care and kindness, they can make a tremendous difference in the lives of students who experience low aim, mediocrity, and disappointment. I know love has the power to heal, transform and make us stronger. You will never exhibit love and care until you go to where your people are. It is said that love is to a thirsty soul what water is to a barren land.

Love has to move us to action! It must demonstrate persistence in pushing aside obstacles. An illustration comes to mind when I think about the power and motivation of love. When a gold miner enters into a mine, a pit or quarry to dig for gold, he is not discouraged or halted because of the astonishing amount of dirt, stone and rock. No! He knows that gold is there. He is motivated, excited, and determined to find the precious gold. Like a classroom teacher or instructional leader, we too are motivated to search out and find the gold in every student. We cannot become paralyzed by the shortfalls or deficiencies of the student or staff member. We have to relentlessly dig, uncover, and find the hidden gifts and talents which we know are present to celebrate and build upon. When we change the way we look at things, the things we look at change. As you lead your school community, are you consumed by and fixated on the dirt? Are you obsessed and preoccupied over your students' shortcomings, brooding over their deficits, overwhelmed and discouraged by their flaws? Or are you driven by the gold — their potential, their strengths, talents, gifts and capabilities? I believe in order to achieve exceptional success in our work, we must learn to discover and focus on what is strong and right with our students and avoid being fixated on what is perceived to be wrong with them. Search for the gold!

This is how Cleo approached and operated in the school and in the classroom. He proceeded in his work with the motivation and eagerness to find each student's strengths and gifts. He focused on what was strong within each one and didn't dwell on what was wrong. He displayed what Norman Vincent Peale states, "To be successful is to be helpful, caring, and constructive, to make everything and everyone you touch a little bit better." As Cleo searched for the gold, he was focused and unwavering. He expressed love in a number of distinct ways as outlined below.

T-I-M-E

Instructional leader: Will you be committed to investing your time in your students, teachers and staff (before school, after school, after practice, during lunch, while chatting in the hallway, in a meeting, before a game, after a game)?

I vividly recall when Cleo took some classmates and me to visit college campuses: Virginia State University (his alma mater), Virginia Union University, and Howard University. He took us to Virginia State University's Homecoming one year, and it was an incredible, life-changing and a defining moment for me. The atmosphere was very electric and contagious. It was full of history, pride and excellence. I was, and still am, very grateful for that experience. It allowed us to envision a more excellent path forward as high school students.

G-I-V-E

Cleo gave us the "Triple A Treatment," as John Maxwell describes. When you give people consistent and sincere *attention*, *affirmation* and *appreciation*, they acquire a greater sense of value and importance. When building relationships with people, begin by giving them your undivided **attention** because when you "pay closer attention, you reduce tension, apprehension and dissension." So give attention!

Affirm people. Focus on their strengths, their importance, their gifts, and their contributions, then observe what happens next. You will be amazed by how positively people will respond. Affirmation is oxygen to the soul! It breathes significance and value into the spirit. Most people are desperate for validation and they want to be acknowledged for the good in them. Effective school leaders understand the power of encouragement. Endorsements are gifts that will never be forgotten and will touch the deepest parts of our very being. When leaders care enough to affirm and validate an individual, they are adding to their personal sense of importance and value. So encourage and affirm people early and often.

Express **appreciation** and gratitude to students and staff generously in your school. These elements are powerful in creating meaningful school relationships and setting up purposeful communication, connection, and collaboration among students, staff and the overall school community. When people feel appreciated and recognized for their work and contributions, they are more likely to be motivated, engaged and productive because of an atmosphere where they feel valued and respected. According to LinkedIn, surveys show that feeling appreciated is the #1 indicator people value most in the work environment. So express authentic appreciation and gratitude frequently.

C-A-R-E

Cleo cared enough to be kind. A kind gesture or word can reach a hurt that only compassion and love can heal. People remember kindness if nothing else, and Cleo Davis displayed these behaviors throughout my high school experience. He represented the love, care and kindness needed to touch and transform my life. As an instructional leader, he exhibited the powerful "love thing" through kindness. Care and kindness are essential to change and elevate lives.

One of my dearest childhood friends from Washington, DC is Mike Johnson (Mickey Boy). His mother, whom I affectionately called Ms. Johnny, died several years ago. She was a victim of Alzheimer's disease. She suffered with this condition for approximately eight years before she passed. In her later years with the disease, she was unable to recognize me, her adopted son, nor her biological sons, Mike and Greg. Mike expressed to me the sadness he felt when she no longer recognized him. She could not even recall his name. Eventually, she slipped away to a sad, dark place where those who suffer with dementia go.

One day, while Mike was visiting his mother at the nursing home, the caregiver stepped out of the room for a moment. Realizing that the caregiver was gone, Ms. Johnny looked around in a confused manner then turned to Mike and asked, "where did the kind lady go?" Mike told her that she would be right back. Isn't it amazing? Ms. Johnny couldn't recognize her own son, but she could recognize kindness in the stranger. Mark Twain once said, "Kindness is the language which the deaf can hear and the blind can see." The significance here is, whenever you have the opportunity to offer kindness, I encourage you to never hold back because everyone you meet is fighting a battle and is experiencing challenges. I implore you to look beyond the masks that students and staff wear. Look beyond their camouflage: their nose rings, tattoos, wild hair color or hairstyles, and outfits, and look within instead.

School leaders, be mindful that love and kindness are never wasted. They always make a difference. They greatly impact the receiver and the giver during given challenges. A gratifying, heartfelt moment occurred one evening for me at church, St. Paul's Baptist Church in Richmond, Virginia. That night, one of my former students (Merrill Gray) whom I had not seen in over 30 years, came up to me and simply made my day even more special. We hugged, became a little emotional, and even a bit tearful. We briefly updated each other on our current lives. He asked if I was on Facebook and I replied yes. This is what he posted the next day that warmed my heart and affirmed my work in education and the power of love and kindness:

> *I attended the concert at St Paul Baptist last night. I'm sitting in the back and I can see an individual who looks very familiar 2 me but I wasn't sure if it was who I thought. I asked an usher 2 walk me over 2 c. This person positively influenced me as a youngster. He loved me, cared 4 me, taught me, punished me, inspired me. I could go on and on. By the way he also coached me. I hadn't seen him in over 30+ years. When he looked at me, he and I both broke into tears and hugged and didn't want to let go. Very clear that after all these years he still loves me the same. Mr William Parker, I love u and u mean the world 2 me. Time stood still for a moment yesterday. Forgot he was a teacher at Henderson Middle*

That is a moment I will cherish forever! I'm sure many of you have experienced the very same joy as an educator. Merrill was a great young man and excellent point guard and leader on Henderson Middle School's basketball team. But let's be clear, he was no saint! He made me earn my money as an educator. Nevertheless, he could have remained in his seat, hidden in the crowd and opted not to come forward that night at church. I would not have known he was even present in the midst of over 1,500 people attending the celebration. But a relationship that was established over 30 years ago prompted him to get out of his seat, come forward and be a blessing to this old man. We have a choice every day when working with young people — to be an SOB (Son of a B...) or SOP (Significant Other Person).

There are numerous books written about leadership and scores of conferences, workshops and webinars you can attend. However, all of the knowledge in the world can't make you an effective leader. It's the love for the work and the love for your school community that influence you to show up. It has to be authentic and at the center of your motivation and purpose. The difference between effective leaders and the less effective leaders is not what they know — it is what they do. Do they behave in a way that demonstrates love and care? Remember, leadership is a two-sided coin.

As the lead torch bearer, standard bearer and lead quality controller for your school, it is essential to create a caring, supportive school community. Place your students and staff ahead of yourself and build a strong sense of connectedness, belongingness, and community. Just remember that "the simple acts of caring and love are heroic" (Edward Albert). Love is the key and will open hearts and doors. As you begin and continue your instructional journey, know that at the core of your work, instructional leadership is a love thing! Everybody needs an angel and a champion, so be that angel and champion by valuing people! Amplify your love! Stand your full weight on choosing to make lives better! Remember love is an action verb and its power in service can transform mediocrity, mud and mess into a miracle. Kindness and love are the things we need most when touching lives. This demonstration of love in service is the rent we pay for living.

"Vision without action is merely a dream. Action without vision just passes the time. Vision with action can change the world."
—Joel Barker

Chapter 2
School Vision

One of the most important elements in lifting a school to new heights is vision — what the leader sees for the future of his students and staff as a school community. Vision is the leader's perception and portrait of the school to come. The school's best version of itself derives in the heart and mind of the leader. John Maxwell believes "that leaders see more than others see and they see it before others see it." Vision tells and foretells of a more dynamic and productive future for a school. It forecasts a new and improved narrative of what a school could become. This new outlook exhibits greater love, a greater sense of community, coherence, adherence, support, care, pride and achievement. This reimagined transformation depicts a golden image of a school, "a school on a hill," thriving, excelling and serving its people in a climate of high expectations, excellence, and equity. A school's vision guides and elevates a school community to come together to lift its students to the highest elevation of being "future ready." So having a vision is vital, and it must be crystal clear for all within the school community to understand and then follow with confidence, certainty and courage. It cannot be clear as mud: fuzzy, vague and filled with indecisions and inconsistencies. It must be distinct and clear to inspire and to require the school community to work collaboratively to lift its students to the highest degree of competency, compassion and responsible citizenship.

A lack of vision reminds me of the Lewis Carroll story, *Alice in Wonderland*. Alice asks the Cheshire Cat who was sitting and resting in a nearby tree, "Would you tell me please, which way I should go from here? What road should I take?" The cat responds, "That depends a good deal on where you want to go. Where do you want to go?" Alice answers, "I don't much care where." So the cat says,

"Then, it really doesn't matter which way you go or what road you take."

An unclear school vision creates enormous challenges and complications that hinder the forward progression and effectiveness of a school. A muddled and incoherent outlook will infect the school with a lack of direction, priorities, goals, poor communication, focus, school alignment and accountability, which are all essential in moving a school forward to reach a clear destination and target. In the words of Yogi Berra, famed baseball player and manager of the New York Yankees, "If you don't know where you are going, you probably aren't going to get there."

A key lesson for administrators to learn is that a hazy, lazy, ambiguous vision offers no clear, definitive direction or purpose, nor will it excite energy toward breakthrough achievement. Additionally, the absence of a clear school vision will persuade staff members to create their own vision and views which may be contrary to, and in conflict with, the leader's direction. So as an instructional leader, it is important to have a school vision which is clear and compelling, so that the school community can get behind it with spirit and support it. The school vision must ignite a fire, a passion within the very soul of the school, and awaken an intensity that creates corporate buy-in and uniformed action.

A school's vision answers the questions:

1. Where are we headed?
2. How are we going to get there?
3. What do we want to become once we've arrived?

As the instructional leader and torchbearer for the school community, your vision must answer these questions and provide clarity and confidence in the direction the school is headed. Leaders with a clear, bold vision spark passion, power and purpose in a school. They understand that nothing great ever happens without enthusiasm and conviction. They know that becoming what you have never been and achieving what you have never done before will require exceptional intensity and commitment.

Merely having a vision or lofty goals is not enough. You must be "sold out," fully immersed and baptized into the very life and character of the vision. Because if you are not fully committed, it will be very difficult to demonstrate what you do not have or do not fully believe. Half-hearted and lukewarm behavior will not achieve anything of substance or quality; only fearless, passionate, determination will! Cecil Beaton encouraged leaders to *"be daring, be different, be impractical, be anything that will assert integrity of purpose and imaginative vision against the play-it-safers, the creatures of the commonplace, the slaves of the ordinary."* Boldness, courage and conviction are what he trumpeted for a vision, but it will take action — bold, fierce and intensive action — to achieve the vision.

Too often leaders build a vision based on the deficiencies and shortcomings that they see rather than a vision of rich possibilities and potential. They allow what they don't have to influence their dreams and hopes about the future. So they live down to limitations and barriers instead of living up to possibilities and promise. Vision is the picture and portrait; but the work — the intentional, focused, hard work will realize the vision. Having a vision but lacking the required behavior will be unproductive and futile. The school leader must provoke the needed actions to accomplish the vision. In the ardent words of John Maxwell, "You must walk the talk, because your walk talk is more powerful and effective than your talk talk."

Jack Welch, former CEO of General Electric stated, "good leaders create a vision, articulate the vision, passionately own the vision and relentlessly drive it to completion." Action always speaks louder than words! The manner in which you behave will reveal how committed and devoted you really are! So what you do or don't do will uncover your true self and belief. The school community may be hesitant and even skeptical of what you say, but they will believe what they see you do; essentially, how you behave in critical situations. Whether you see the vision as achievable or not, your inner beliefs and thoughts will be exposed over time. Additionally, if there is anyone on your staff or team who doesn't know what the vision of the school is, and what is essential to the school, they will ultimately fall far short of what is expected and required to achieve it. Their contribution will be minimal and mediocre at best! Not only that, but they will actually hinder, cripple and even sabotage the team and the school from achieving the desired success.

Reverend Dr. Lance Watson, Pastor of St. Paul's Baptist Church in Richmond, VA, used this illustration to capture the core of what a vision is all about in a sermon:

> *On top of a jigsaw puzzle box is the complete picture of what the puzzle will look like once it is assembled. When you first open the jigsaw puzzle box, all of the pieces fall out in disorder. They are mixed up, jumbled and scattered. As you focus on the image on the box and begin the process of putting the fragments together, it is not uncommon to experience some frustration, irritation and exasperation. Connecting these oddly shaped remnants takes time, energy, concentration and a great deal of collaboration to achieve the identified picture (vision) on the box top. The image on top of the box keeps everyone glued and fixed until the picture is fully realized.*

My takeaway from that sermon is that a church and a school are both like a jigsaw puzzle. There are several unique pieces that need to be assembled and interlocked to achieve the complete vision. Both the leader and the team need a clear, unifying picture, a focal point, guiding everyone towards its destination and ambition.

Dr. Mark Edwards, the 2013 National Superintendent of the Year and former Superintendent of Danville City in Virginia, Henrico County in Virginia and Mooresville, North Carolina, was passionate about the vision of Mooresville Graded School District becoming the #1 Performing School District in NC as measured by state standards and becoming a nationally recognized school district. Mooresville was ranked thirty-eight out of one-hundred and fifteen school districts when he first arrived in 2007. The staff primarily received his vision and aspirations as "superintendent talk" — just what superintendents are expected to say to a new staff. They initially considered his lofty views as "window dressing, varnish and fluff." But in the following days, weeks and months, they observed something totally different about this leader. This superintendent's daily actions, laser-like focus, conversations, decisions, strong sense of accountability, passion, and commitment to high student achievement were relentless. His actions and behaviors expressed priorities. His vision and expectations served as a clarion call to action, purpose and a need for consistency. As a result, in 2011, Mooresville soared to #2 in NC, second only to Chapel Hill. It took Mooresville four years to become an overnight success!

The school district's motto of "Every Child, Every Day" caught fire and captured the imagination and spirit of the entire school district. Not only were we #2 in NC, but were also #1 in the state in attaining the highest Annual Measurable Objectives. Additionally, we ranked #1 in the graduation rate for African-American students with 95% up from 67% five years earlier. The overall graduation rate was third in the state and 88% of the graduating seniors were attending college. Dr. Edwards' "High Fives," as I call them, were key practices in establishing buy-in for the vision.

#1 - **Inclusivity.** This required telling the district's story wrapped in a culture of love and care with a moral obligation of expecting and demonstrating excellence, fairness, and equity among all of its demographics. We could not have reached a 90 plus percent success rate as a district with White children or affluent children alone. We could not have reached excellence or had fundamental fairness in our school community if we did not expect all of our students to succeed at high levels of achievement. We expected our teachers to teach "Every Child, Every Day," not "Some of the Children, Some of the Time." We had to behave as if we believed that all students had the capacity to learn at high levels. Dr.

Edwards expected us to close the achievement gap and to be inclusive in our Talented and Gifted classes, AP courses, other rigorous courses, student leadership representation, and hiring practices, among other areas. He was keenly aware that institutional racism was still alive and well in Mooresville. The school system had to lead the way and be the example for the entire township with fairness and inclusion. His leadership, heart, and vision confronted this head on. In his words, "if you can't help them see the light (vision) then help them feel the heat." It did not matter whether he was speaking to the town's Economic Development Council, Chamber of Commerce, Rotary Club, Lowe's Corporation, NAACP, or Black Ministerial Alliance. In any instance, he stayed on message and was true to the vision. It was about healing and lifting, not blocking or hindering segments of our school community.

#2 - **Communication**. Dr. Edwards talked it up every day and at every opportunity. He made time and created opportunities to communicate the vision with key players, teams, and all stakeholders through school meetings, planning sessions, retreats, community meetings, workshop trainings, data meetings, newsletters, posters, emails, focus teams, and the district's tv productions. Through these outlets, he ensured that there was an alignment in the goals of each school, each team, and every individual within the district's vision.

#3 - **Teamwork**. Dr. Edwards took time to develop, invest in and empower his teams from his central office cabinet, to his principals, assistant principals and teacher leaders. Building leadership capacity was key in nurturing the vision. "Whenever the vision and challenges of the organization escalate, teamwork must elevate," as John Maxwell states.

#4 - **Rewards System**. Dr. Edwards fostered excitement, motivation, and engagement around the vision by articulating the WIFM (What's In It For Me?) Model. He realized that people want to be a part of a winning team, something really special. He communicated how we would all benefit from embracing the vision. He explained and reinforced the rewards when the goals of the vision were realized, such as state and national recognition, increased public confidence in the work and the product of the district, the city's economic development impact, career development opportunities and financial rewards.

#5 - **Praise**. The team celebrated meaningful benchmarks and achievements along the way. People are our most valuable resource. They can take the vision to a touchdown or fumble and drop the ball before crossing the goal line. How that vision is cultivated can either create enthusiasm and excitement or resistance and struggle. What is vital to understand is the devotion to become something you've never been and achieving something we've never done! Build on the Magic of Momentum and Good News!

As a result of these "High Fives," the school district was featured in national magazines such as *The Wall Street Journal* and *Scholastic News*, plus featured on Fox News, on Public Broadcasting Station (PBS), and awarded the Sylvia Charp Award for its Digital Conversion, to name a few. With this publicity, there was a steady stream of visitors from more than 40 states and countries visiting the district. One of its many visitors was President Barack Obama in 2013.

Show me a leader or a team without vision and conviction and I'll show you a school that is ineffective and unproductive in serving its school community. There are far too many schools with low aim who play it safe instead of seeking the spectacular. There are far too many schools that aim for the easy instead of the exceptional. There are far too many schools that target the typical rather than the tremendous. There are far too many schools that focus on the familiar instead of the fantastic! Even a turtle sticks his head out in order to move forward.

Instructional leader, I encourage you to find your vision and let it guide your steps and your actions, and also encourage your heart. Allow the vision to give your school community something phenomenal to guide them to an extraordinary reputation to achieve and uphold. Remember, it's all about vision — what the leader sees for the future of his students and staff as a school community. This, my friend, is a "love thing!" It is being sold out, fully committed, and engaged to achieve the inspiring and the exciting while moving your school and school district forward.

"Kindness is the most powerful, least costly, and most underrated agent of human change."
— Bob Kerrey

Chapter 3
Creating a Community of Caring

Creating a community of caring is a love thing! There is substantial research affirming the importance, need, and the benefits of becoming a school community of caring. Both the challenge and the goal in the schools that I led were to create a place where love, care, and a high regard for students, staff and parents would be evident in the culture of the school and in the way we value people. Everyone in our school was expected to be treated as valued individuals who deserved our investment of consecrated effort, encouragement, support and respect to achieve at higher levels. In a school of caring, we want students to consistently experience and encounter love, support, kindness, encouragement and discipline (instruction).

As leaders, we believed that transformation takes place in the heart. As such, our journey to change our school started there — in the heart and soul of the adults. The adults in the building had to become agents of kindness and change in order for us to achieve at desired levels. Love and kindness had to be substantive and real on our campus. It had to be felt in the lives of our young people and our staff. Albert Schweitzer once said, "Constant kindness can accomplish much. As the sun makes ice melt, kindness causes misunderstanding, mistrust, and hostility to evaporate." It was love and discipline (instruction) which placed us on a path to becoming a more excellent school for our students and staff to learn and grow.

As a school, we relied heavily on soul power, safety, synergy, support, trust and high expectation to facilitate exceptional growth. These essential elements were necessary in Henrico High School becoming a school community of caring, which catapulted our students and staff to acquire full accreditation and national recognition honors. We began with kindness and love, our "Soul

Power." We believed that compassion displayed in action would be contagious and would change students' outlook, and ultimately, change their outcome. In the most challenging and difficult school settings, kindness can never be wasted. It has the power to transform the dynamics and character of a school, one random act of kindness at a time.

After much discussion and collaboration with the staff, our school embarked on a mission to reexamine, revise, and revamp our expectations and practices. The more we began to understand who we served, the better we could serve them. Our school could not become what we needed it to be as long as we remained stuck in allowing our biases and low expectations to taint our actions. We needed to desperately change. In the words of Tony Robbin, "If you do what you've always done, you'll get what you've always gotten." Therefore, if we wanted different results, then we had to behave differently. The school leaders on campus had to set an example; we had to make a change.

Listed below are some of the important common sense action steps we employed to extend kindness, love and discipline (instruction) to start us on a new path.

Soul Power
As school leaders, we acknowledged early on that if we wanted the school to change and become more responsive, then change had to begin with us. We had to lead from within our spirit to impact and influence how we would now do business. The administrative team and teacher leaders emphasized and encouraged our staff to take a close, hard look at our behavior and ask the questions: *Is our conduct a hurdle, a hindrance, to the school's progress, learning climate and student achievement? Are our beliefs and attitudes, how we treat and talk to students, our hidden biases and prejudices partly the cause of some of our problems?* If we wanted to create a more conducive and productive learning environment, we had to look inwardly, within our clusters, cliques and inner circles to confer, confront, challenge, call out, rethink, reevaluate and reassess our practices, policies and approaches toward our students.

Our students were struggling with a number of intense, deep and challenging issues. Considering such, our behavior as a staff could not add affliction nor anguish to their lives. The high school years are especially important in helping students to manage their emotions and their circumstances. These years can be brutal! As leaders, we had to be an epicenter of care, support, guidance and change. Many students were navigating through a maze of uncertainty trying to decipher life after high school — whether to work, join the military, or attend college. In the midst of navigating the unknown, they were also faced with significant roadblocks, like social media influences, drug and alcohol use, bullying, and matters of the heart with respect to romantic relationships and encounters, just to name a few. Our students needed kind and caring adults to listen and offer support. They needed advocates who would encourage them to press on!

As a school, we made a concerted effort to:

- ***Remember students and call them by their name.*** Calling students by their name communicates respect and helps students feel recognized as valued individuals. We had to employ a laser-like focus to identify those students who tend to be overlooked, ignored, forgotten and neglected. The importance in a caring school is to ensure that each student is known by a caring adult, especially the so-called "least of these, the left outs and the lost ones."

- ***Build relationships with students to promote a positive learning environment.*** We made a point to know our students as individuals. We listened to their stories and got to know their interests, ambitions, challenges, and their goals. When a school seeks to understand its students, it shows them that they care. We desired to care enough to be kind. William Arthur Ward describes building relationships with the impact of love: "Flatter me, and I may not believe you. Criticize me, and I may not like you. Ignore me, and I may not forgive you. Encourage me, and I will not forget you. Love me and I may be forced to love you."

We made genuine efforts to establish positive relationships and connections with our students. It was a must for us!

- ***Give attention to students.*** This is one of the foundational gifts that can be given in a caring community. Recognizing and acknowledging students will foster a strong sense of value and respect. Will Schwalbe once said, "The greatest gift you can give anyone is your undivided attention." Attention is recognition and an expression of caring. It affirms value and worth in students. All of us seek, in some form or fashion, attention from someone who matters. I believe, especially in schools, when we pay closer attention to our students and colleagues, we reduce and lower tension, contention and dissension in our relationships and in the school setting. So be alert and give ample attention and focus to the people around you. Be in the present because there is an urgency of now to be available.

One of the uncomplicated and simplest ways school leaders can improve and promote a caring community is to recognize and reinforce the good things students do on campus on a regular basis. For example, give praise to students, especially in front of their peers. Write a note, use PA announcements, make positive telephone calls, send emails or texts to parents, encourage teachers to post students' names in the classroom for achievement or for being positive, helpful, or resilient.

Our administration posted student pictures in our cafeterias for *Random Acts of Kindness*. These were students who went out of their way to help fellow students and staff on campus; helped a handicapped or injured student to maneuver their way to class; assisted a new student around campus; helped a staff member carry resources from his/her car to the classroom; expressed gratitude and appreciation to our bus drivers, custodial, maintenance or cafeteria staff; volunteered to participate in community service projects on campus after school or on the weekends; welcomed and assisted guests and visitors on campus; alerted staff that a friend or classmate was having a very difficult time at home or at school; prevented conflicts and disruptions on campus by making staff aware of potential problems; picked up fellow students for Saturday School;

and tutored fellow students in a subject area. These are just a few of the examples of kindness that we recognized and highlighted. I can recall a student who found a wallet in the parking lot one day full of cash and submitted it to the office. Not a dollar was missing. What an example of honesty and decency! This positive behavior, and other similar expressions of kindness, were exactly the examples we were trying to reinforce.

"Catching students doing right" was our approach in shifting the atmosphere on campus and changing the image of the school. We believed that positive behavior, when acknowledged and celebrated, had the greater chance of being reinforced and repeated. It was a part of our belief to praise in public and counsel and correct in private! As a school, we chose to focus and intensify what was strong and right with our students rather than to underscore what was wrong with them. We chose to stir up the gifts, not feed and underline the negative.

Here is how we did it and how you can do it too!

- ***Communicate appreciation to students.*** This is another key building block in developing a caring community. Receiving appreciation is a fundamental human need. William James, well-known psychologist and philosopher, once said, "The deepest principle of human nature is a craving to be appreciated." When we show appreciation to our students, their regard and respect for us will grow and so will our influence as their teacher or school leader. When there are authentic demonstrations of appreciation, students will feel special about what they do and what they have accomplished. Experiencing appreciation makes students feel better about themselves and optimistic about their future. Acknowledgment and appreciation encourage students to move forward with increased energy and resilience. Students will work harder and extend themselves more if they know that they will be recognized for their progress and achievement. Show appreciation to students early and often. It will have a tremendous impact.

- ***Seek opportunities to affirm students.*** Affirmation is another critical component in a caring community. When school leaders express compassion and support to students with statements like, "I believe in you, I trust you, I care about you, I am counting on you, I know you can do it," nothing is more uplifting and heartfelt. A kind word or a warm gesture can reach a hurt, a pain, that only kindness and love can touch and heal. Students remember kindness if nothing else. Maya Angelou said it best: "I've learned that people forget what you said, people will forget what you did, but people will never forget how you made them feel." The reality is, students are starving for validation and they want to be acknowledged for the good in them.

- ***Help students win by being an extraordinary encourager.*** The word encourage means to urge forward, to give support, confidence and hope. Acts of kindness and inspiration are never forgotten. Every student needs an adult in the schoolhouse to help them achieve their dreams and goals. They need someone who sees the gifts and talents in them that they can't see in themselves. These adults have the ability to stir up the gifts within their students, urging them to stretch beyond their comfort zone. A single word of encouragement from a caring adult can give a student the confidence he or she needs to overcome the obstacles and obstructions in their path and take the necessary steps toward a more productive future. Whether students need help in achieving success on the state assessments; a written letter of recommendation for a job, college entrance application, or scholarship; support so a student can remain in school and not drop out; a wake-up call to get them up in the morning for school; making arrangements for a student to eat school breakfast or lunch; finding resources within the school or outside of the school for respective assistance; helping a student practice for an interview; finding a tutor for extra help; paying for senior fees, field trip costs, dresses or tuxedos for prom, or something else, these acts of kindness all demonstrate forms of encouragement. When a student shares their hopes, dreams and goals with you, and you assist them in making their dreams and goals a reality, you've made a special impression and connection for life. Many student successes are greatly attributed to a caring school leader or teacher who believed in their students, told them they could achieve, and then helped them to do so. This behavior is a hallmark of a community of caring.

Safety

Safety is an underrated element in creating a community of caring. While Principal of Henrico High, our Superintendent, Dr. Mark Edwards, had a conversation with me outlining his marching orders as I approached my first year: 1) Become fully accredited; 2) Improve the learning climate by developing a safe and orderly school environment; and 3) Increase the use of technology on campus.

Dr. Edwards' clearly communicated goals came as no surprise. As educational leaders, we understood from the onset that in order for us to meet his expectations, we had to get a handle on our learning environment and protect and shield students and staff from physical, emotional, and psychological harm. We had to drastically reduce the constant acts of disruptions, distractions and disharmony on campus. So we embarked on a quest to create a learning environment that produced a healthy, supportive setting for both students and staff that led to full school accreditation in our first leadership year. School safety became everyone's responsibility and everyone's business. Teamwork truly made the dream work!

In order to successfully meet this goal, collecting and analyzing data and meeting with key stakeholders to assess the best course of action was essential. No one was exempt from these meetings. We engaged with the administrative team, key teacher leaders, school counselors, the security team, resource officers, student leaders, central office school safety specialists and PTA representatives. During these meetings, we acquired input and began the creation of a school plan and approach. We collaborated and worked diligently to set up a clearly defined system of schoolwide expectations and standards, school policies, procedures, structures, and both a student reward system to reinforce appropriate behavior and a system to curb inappropriate conduct. We knew that it would take everybody, every day, enforcing all the rules and standards all of the time.

We revised and strengthened our student, teacher and staff handbooks which conveyed the expectations and rules holding the school community accountable for behavior and conduct. Our direction was to ensure that the entire school community operated in a smooth and orderly manner. The handbooks had clearly defined guidelines and agreements set up for the management and governance of the school. The handbooks protected the rights of students and teachers and outlined the responsibilities, obligations, and expectations for students and staff alike. The handbooks were prepared for the purpose of keeping students and faculty/staff members informed of expectations surrounding attendance, announcements, the Pledge of Allegiance, assemblies, calendar of events, classroom management, homework and the use of textbooks, arrival to and departure from school, copyright, emergency procedures, grading, and hall passes. It further outlined injury and illness on campus, the use of cell phones and electronics, parent/teacher conferences and contacts, snow days and school delays, dress code, and school visitors.

The handbooks described how the school would operate and conduct business as an organization. It served as a guide to advance our mission and to place the school in the best possible position to be more productive toward our march to accreditation. We understood that if we lacked guidance and structure, our school setting would be ripe for continued turmoil, turbulence and tension. Ultimately, we selected a dedicated committee that was tasked with revising the student handbook, which was led by an assistant principal. The committee included input from school counselors, a PTA representative, and student representatives.

These school policies, procedures and standards were not only about keeping students and staff safe, but also about promoting fairness and excellence. Henrico High School had to provide clear policies and procedures to guide the day-to-day operations within the school. These school policies and standards were important because they established the quality for learning and safety, as well as accountability and direction. Without these substantive, procedural structures in place, the handbooks would lack the guidance and function necessary to provide for the educational needs of students and staff. In addition to the handbooks, teaching the County's Code of Conduct was extremely important in creating a safe, secure and welcoming environment for all students of Henrico High School. It was critical that the school division and the school's expectations were clear to students, families, staff and the community.

Together, each stakeholder had a vital role to play to ensure a safe and supportive learning environment for our students and staff. To this end, we stressed and taught the District's Student Code of Conduct to our students during the first week of school to make our expectations, standards, and consequences very clear. We wanted to "begin with the end in mind" of creating a positive learning community. We also administered a digital Student Code of Conduct Assessment created by our Safety Team to appraise and reinforce the knowledge and understanding of our students about the Student Code of Conduct. In addition, handbooks of the District's Student Code of Conduct were mailed to each student household. Once the parents received the document, they were expected to review the Student Code of Conduct with their child(ren), sign the back page of the booklet and return it to school. This provided an added layer of accountability.

<u>Transition</u>
After strengthening our handbooks and developing the safety and school climate plan, we met with the entire faculty and staff to convey our collective work going forward in facilitating a safer and orderly school environment. Emphasizing, once again, it would take everybody, every day, to enforce all of the expectations and rules all of the time! This strong belief meant that persistence and proper supervision on campus were a must to minimize and reduce negative climate issues. The proactive expectation of "All Hands on Deck" during student transition was the school charge!

Henrico High was a campus-style school with eighteen buildings to supervise. It was our non-negotiable expectation that during morning intake, in the classroom, between classes and during any student transition, during school lunches, special assemblies, afternoon dismissal, after-school activities and sporting events, that adequate supervision was present. I informed the entire school faculty and staff that it would take all of us working diligently daily to turn the tide and make a difference in campus life. From the first day of school in September to the last of October, we had to be relentless and unbending to establish a "beachhead" on campus.

We understood that our school climate would move in stages from forming, storming, norming to performing (Tuckman, 1965). If we truly desired to escape the grip of excessive school conflicts, mediocrity and poor student conduct, we had to quickly ascend to the level of "norming" where students and staff were accepting and meeting the required standards and establishing new norms. If we failed to build momentum by the end of October and shift to a new and improved normal, we would continually struggle and encounter disturbances, disorder and chaos throughout the school year. We would not place our students or school in the best position to win and perform well on district, state or national assessments. We could not advance our school if we remained stuck and paralyzed in a school level of "storming." A critical mass of teamwork, caring and collaboration was the only way to move the mission forward to accomplish it.

Just because we desired positive outcomes and expected consistency from the staff didn't mean it was going to happen, however. Previous administrations had required the same but experienced inconsistencies, shortcomings and gaps in supervision. To ensure the consistency of "All Hands On Deck," we employed a number of actions to make this expectation stick. Our collective mindset was to be insistent. We wanted the school's learning environment to change and improve so we needed to be resolute and steadfast. Our school life would only get better through our enduring and uncompromising actions, which included:

> **1.** We expected the administrative team to set the example by being visible, vigilant and active on the walkways during each transition. This expectation and pattern of behavior influenced and modeled to our staff the importance of uniting to improve the safety and order of our school. We learned over the years that people are more willing and inclined to do what they see their leaders do. When leadership models the way and represents what is expected, they strengthen and bolster the desired collective action to bring about change. The day-to-day examples of the administrative team out front

leading the way forged movement and energy to be consistent. Our position was to be intentional and determined, not casual or occasional. We reminded administrators by radio, five minutes prior to transitions, to quickly wrap up whatever they were doing, to report promptly to their designated area of supervision, and be conspicuous and noticeable. The leadership could not inspect what they were expected to if they were chained in their office or MIA (Missing In Action).

Leaders are responsible for their people's performance. To ensure we had "All Hands On Deck," the administration had to be in place to affirm that this action was indeed happening throughout campus. We understood that what gets measured gets done! It started with the principal and the administration. We had to be in position to hold the line on staff behaviors, contrary to school expectations, and we needed to model expected behavior and standards! Appropriate and consistent reinforcement of supervision was expected by teachers and administrators. Conversations and correspondences were used to either affirm staff for their faithfulness, support, and teamwork, or to address and correct inconsistent or inappropriate behavior. Our steadfast execution and follow-through as a team were needed to make the "All Hands On Deck" expectation stick and lift our school culture.

2. In addition to being present on the walkway, we insisted our teachers have their antennas up. Whether on the walkway, at the threshold of their classroom door, or within the four corners of their classroom, they were expected to be vigilant. We urged them to scan and read the faces of their students – the students who were near them on the walkway, the ones who passed by or those who entered into their classroom. Our ability as a school to observe and read facial expressions and body language helped us pick up on students' unspoken issues or negative feelings that they might have. This required a high level of observation, with both eyes and ears, for signs of anger, frustration or sadness. We also urged them to pay close attention to any elevated noise, disturbances, or inappropriate conversations which could lead to a disruption or conflict. With consistency and diligence, our staff was able to pick up on and distinguish between appropriate, acceptable student excitement versus activity from troubling annoyances and possible clashes.

3. We made periodic and strategic PA announcements prior to the transition of classes reminding students of the importance of arriving promptly to their next class, its benefits, and the consequences of not arriving on time. The announcement also reiterated the expectation of students to be sitting on "GO," by immediately taking a seat in class and engaging in the teacher's "warm-up" activity.

Furthermore, we stressed the importance of our legal responsibility of providing adequate supervision in the classrooms and on campus. We reminded our teachers and school leaders that we were acting in the place of parents, so it was imperative that we supervised in a responsible, attentive, and reasonable manner to prevent and minimize off-task student behaviors, disturbances, acts of violence or injuries.

Our presence in the classrooms, consistent surveillance, attentiveness, preparedness, planning, student engagement, relationships with students, and proximity control were key and essential to enhance safety and promote a positive learning climate. However, in order to really create and sustain a safe school community, we had to care enough to address the safety and orderly aspects of the learning environment by ensuring that we set clear expectations, be proactive and vigilant, and persistently insist upon uniform and consistent supervision on campus.

4. Caring leaders see things differently. They gaze through a leadership lens influenced and driven by love, compassion, and service. They understand the tremendous value and worth of people, even when their treasures and gifts are hidden and buried deep within. Leaders don't just believe it or say it; they do it! Love and kindness motivate them to be concerned and to seek answers and solutions. School leaders organize and mobilize their people, their teams and their resources to meet the multiple and demanding needs of their students and staff. This ensures that the focus is on the main goal: that student learning is the fundamental purpose.

A caring school, immersed in love, positions itself to serve with a greater purpose, a higher mission, and a fervent spirit of "can do." School leaders look internally at what they already have on campus — that which is within their reach and within their sphere of influence. School leaders utilize those resources to increase their impact and to spark the momentum necessary to turn negative, adverse school trends and realities around. These trends and realities most often include high student absences, low student achievement, and a disorderly, disruptive and discouraging school atmosphere. Leaders believe it is vital and wise to tap into and harness what is closest to students, and that, my friend, are the adults on campus! Building "esprit de corps," a sense of family and team, which are essential and paramount for school reform.

School leaders, as a matter of lift and focus, give their staff and students a positive and more favorable image and reputation to strive for and to uphold. It is creating a deeper regard and an emotional connection and attachment with the school. In our case at Henrico High School, it was belonging to and standing proudly with the "Warrior Nation" and passionately shouting our slogan and battle cry, "Behold the Green and Gold!" When caring leadership combined with exceptional energy were released, the school environment began to shift, rebrand, and recalibrate. There appeared to be a calm, cool breeze blowing on campus that both the students and staff felt.

The ethos of the school began to change when we developed a more comprehensive, responsive school support system exhibiting a tremendous desire to increase student engagement and student-teacher relationships. As administration, we acknowledged and honed in on this observation to fully maximize our support. School leaders, along with faculty and staff, analyzed data, and identified and communicated student needs. Progressively, we collaborated, challenged, and expected everyone to be a part of the solution by shouldering their responsibilities. We expected staff to walk the talk and convey the essential messages to students that they are valued, respected, and supported. The expectation for staff to build relationships and connect with students was the standard because doing so set the table and the climate for learning.

When seeking to expand their reach and touch on campus, school leaders should consider including bus drivers, cafeteria workers, custodians, maintenance workers and clerical staff. It is my belief that anyone can be a warm, respectful, kind, encouraging person with a listening ear. With a little effort, anyone can get to know students' names and when they sense a concern can inform a teacher or administrator for additional support. The bus driver is the first school staff member to see and hear students in the morning and the last to see and hear them in the afternoon. Their insight and support is crucial.

To further expand on relationship building, consider establishing a mentorship program. Many students grow up having to grapple with academic, personal and social issues. Early intervention and support through a structured mentoring program may be able to provide the encouragement, tools and guidance they need to manage these challenges. At Henrico High School, we initiated a mentoring program called *Each One, Reach One*. In our urban-flavored school, we urged each adult to embrace at least one student to personally connect with, to be watchful over, and to encourage and demonstrate care and concern. We created a list of students we believed needed additional love, attention and support. This list began with our truancy students, our newly transferred students, our students on the economic margins, ESL students, our Muslim students, our LGBTQ+ students, and students who appeared to have difficulty connecting with others. It was fundamental for us to connect and relate with these students in particular and convey care, kindness and a sense of belonging. This strategy, combined with others, helped to increase our average daily attendance rate, graduation rate, our SOL achievement rate, and our overall academic success rate. The mentoring program was also instrumental in the reduction of our student drop-out rate, violence on campus, and out-of-school suspension rate.

Moreover, when I served as the Executive Director for Secondary Schools and Career and Technical Education in Mooresville Graded School District, North Carolina, we created a student mentoring program called *Changing A Life*. This relationship focused on the needs of identified at-promised youth and encouraged them to develop to their fullest potential. The mission of the Mooresville Graded School District mentoring program was to encourage and support students to become successful academically, personally, and socially. There were approximately three-hundred mentor/mentee match-ups in Mooresville. Some of our mentors included the Superintendent of Schools, central office personnel, school staff, including principals, administrators, counselors, teachers, custodial and maintenance workers, the Mooresville's Police Chief, School Resource Officers, School Board members, City Council members, members of the NAACP, Black Ministerial Alliance, and a number of business owners in the community.

This initiative, I believe, was key in the district affirming the message and providing evidence that "we care and we believe in the (so called) least of these." The *Changing A Life Mentoring Program* added guidance and kindness to students who really needed a boost in encouragement and support. The mentors' sense of mission and ability to add value and influence to their mentee helped in increasing our graduation rate, student success rate in the classroom, average daily attendance and the reduction of our suspension rate.

In addition, the administration took appropriate steps to examine and elevate the counseling department services to students, teachers and parents. School leaders should carefully review the job descriptions of their counselors, social workers, school psychologists and other support personnel. Begin with discussions about their understanding of their responsibilities and their work performance, then listen to their ideas and plans to better serve and support students. School leaders, in partnership with the counseling department, are urged to analyze the student data together and then determine school needs. Set priorities and develop an improvement plan, aligned with district and state standards and the school's mission to increase all students' academic achievement as they prepare for an ever-changing world.

Frequently reviewing student results and outcomes must become a part of early warning signals to identify students who are struggling, failing or experiencing difficulty. Armed with this information, school counselors should be in a stronger position to discuss and recommend intervention and support services that would help students succeed at higher levels. The support services department of the school is a vital and integral part of the total educational program. It must not work in isolation, but in collaboration. The department is expected to behave in a proactive manner to target support that would improve students' well-being and their academic success. School leaders must have and meet the expectation to work closely with the support staff to increase their visibility, availability, and accountability.

Group counseling is an important part of the school counseling program and serves as another way to focus support and direct services to students. It has a positive effect on academic, career and social/emotional development and should be supported by the school administration. Group counseling involves a number of students working on shared tasks or specific topics, such as anger management, stress management, student skills development, grief and loss, and conflict resolution. Counseling groups lend themselves to strengthening and developing supportive relationships, camaraderie and positive student connections, as well as academic, career and social/emotional developmental issues and situational concerns. With such an intense focus on student well-being and success, school leaders must work intently with counselors to ensure that students are served appropriately under the college-and-career readiness initiatives. Support services must also become the champion of the students who work with teachers, administrators and parents to widen the net in recommending and enrolling more students, especially underserved students in more rigorous courses traditionally overlooked and discounted.

One strategy to convey the care and visibility of the counseling staff — and to extend proactive support for students — is school leaders requiring counselors to rotate and spend at least thirty minutes in the cafeteria during lunch periods to increase their availability to check-in and follow-up with students. We had three lunch periods at Henrico High, each thirty-five minutes in length between two cafeterias. This approach was an intentional and deliberate way to get ahead on student-related issues by scheduling more adults in areas that allowed students a chance to briefly talk, provide updates, give a heads-up, or to set up another time to further the conversation with a counselor.

Additionally, counselors could be a support to students who were assigned to the In-School- Suspension (ISS) Program. By assigning counselors to this program, this intervention provided an opportunity to add another voice to talk with students about their decisions and how to select a more excellent way in going forward. Counselors are so valuable and needed in various capacities of overall academic success. Some areas where they excel are in offering guidance with conflict resolution, how to improve grades, organizing resources, conducting meetings with teachers, strengthening study skills, connecting students to a school group, club, organization or team, discussing their graduation pace and date, future plans beyond high school, along with other personal and academic related matters. It was our view that we meet students where they were — whether in the cafeteria, on the walkway, in ISS, or at athletic events. We were keenly aware that we must be more visible and available to our students.

Another support service that proved to be pivotal in our increased student achievement was providing extra help opportunities for students who were experiencing difficulty in the classroom. This is what Henrico High School did better than any high school in Henrico County, Virginia. As a school, we had to respond with one voice and only one option as prescribed in the Rick DuFour Model. When students struggled or were failing, we decided as a school to provide extra time and extra instruction. We would not water down our curriculum standards nor did we believe in excessive failures. We also did not want to begin an aggressive campaign of identifying these students as needing exceptional education services. Instead, we offered, as a school, an Early Bird tutoring program to those students who were able to get to school by 7:30 am. We did not offer transportation for the Early Bird tutoring program, however. Students either drove themselves, carpooled, or were dropped off by their parents. We also had a number of our teachers who availed themselves to offer this additional help during this period. One in particular was our varsity basketball coach, Vance Harmon, who taught US History. He had between five to twenty students waiting at his classroom door when he arrived each morning. As a coach, many of his afternoons were filled with coaching duties and preparation for games. Still, he committed his mornings to coaching students academically where needed before school.

While not every teacher participated in the Early Bird tutoring sessions, there were others who provided extra help throughout the day. Teachers were expected to provide at least forty minutes per week during their planning period for targeted students. These were the students who were struggling based on our two-week common assessments. We wanted to provide frequent interventions for those students to avoid time and instructional gaps. Our department chairs had a duty period to provide extra help to identified students and to monitor and collaborate with teachers.

Moreover, we had a strong and comprehensive after-school tutoring program with activity buses each Tuesday, Wednesday and Thursday. Teachers used their common assessment data to invite students to participate, held conferences with them to discuss their individual results, contacted parents to inform them of the need for their child to participate, and included participation incentives. Our content department chairs, in addition to the assistant principal for the department, developed a tutoring schedule with teacher input. We urged our content teachers to plan and offer at least one day a week to tutor after school.

Additionally, we also conducted Saturday School from 9:00 am to 12:00 noon twice a month from February to the end of May. Academic teachers, including our exceptional education teachers, were encouraged to join in the "fun" at least once a month. Transparently, when the opportunity was first presented to staff, we received some push back and some refusal. Several teachers expressed that they were unable to commit for personal reasons. We did not mandate their participation, but strongly encouraged their involvement and engagement. As we gathered student data from our two-week common assessments from each teacher, we continued to see pockets of low student performances from certain teachers. As it was our practice after analyzing data, we sat down with these teachers to gain their perspectives and their plans to implement something different to get better results and measurable improvements. The administration and department chairs offered encouragement, support, guidance and direction as we collaborated to increase student achievement to our desired targets.

If students continued to struggle, however, we had to provide additional time and instructional support. Continuing with low student results was unacceptable! We had to collaborate and find a way forward. These collaborative efforts looked like examining their participation in the Early Bird sessions and exploring extra help opportunities during the school day, after school and during Saturday School. The teacher, content area chair, department chair, and assistant principal had to continue "pushing and lifting" toward stronger teamwork, collaboration and commitment.

"Commitment and consistency in action spark momentum and momentum is a leader's best friend" (John Maxwell). As we progressed through our Saturday School sessions, we observed and documented more and more students and teachers participating. We were averaging 280 students attending our Saturday School prior to state testing with a high of 375 students. Only 50 students had attended our first Saturday School! This was so encouraging! The naysayers were betting on no one showing up! What was so helpful in gaining participation from all core teachers in the early days of our Saturday School Program were the students who attended Saturday School asking for their respective teachers and questioning why they were not available. We gathered this information and shared it with the missing teachers and you guessed it – it became more personal to them. The students wanted extra help, and, ideally they wanted it from the teacher who knew them best. And of course, these teachers cared about the students who sat in their classrooms Monday through Friday and about their individual achievements and futures.

Our teacher attendance in the Saturday School Program was boosted by the outstanding involvement, energy, and success from teachers and students. This reality made it very difficult for teachers to decline participation. Everyone wanted to be a part of this community. It was truly something special and relevant which ultimately closed the academic gaps and provided students with increased competence and confidence going forward.

Our focus and behavior in creating a caring school community helped us transform our school learning climate. The key to our reformation and success heated up in the hearts and souls of the incredible staff who embraced the challenge of becoming agents of change. Our campus became a place where love, kindness, and a high regard for our students, staff and our parents became more real and evident. Because of the fixed focus and acute application of soul power, safety and support, a more caring and supportive school emerged. These crucial components helped to establish a positive learning environment and nurtured exceptional growth which led to full accreditation and national recognition honors.

"They may forget what you said, but they will never forget how you made them feel."
— Carl W. Buehner

Chapter 4
Building Relationships

"Love can't be the fruit until love is at the root!" Rev. Dr. Lance Watson

Relationships are fundamental in creating an effective and caring school community. All significant accomplishments in any school happen because of the connection and synergy developed among its people. Building relationships is a love thing and serves as the core and soul of the direction and work of the school! Love is the key ingredient that makes the difference in a school. It fuels the school's spirit, service, and capacity. As such, the building of positive relationships starts in the heart of the leader. As a school leader, you must focus on creating a caring community, building genuine connections, and displaying sincere concern and love to staff and students. This can only occur when the school leader places a high value and premium on people.

Building positive relationships will involve spending time together, sharing, giving, listening, and supporting one another. These actions lay the groundwork for team engagement and the building of trust and dependability. You can learn a lot by listening to and spending time with the people you work with, your students, staff, parents, and other stakeholders. In the book, *The Wisdom of the Bullfrog: Leadership Made Simple But Not Easy,* by Admiral William H. McRaven, he cites Pope Francis who once said, "A shepherd must smell like his sheep!" I translate that to mean a leader must not be cooped up, confined and isolated in the office, distant and unavailable to his people; instead, a school leader must be consistently visible, engaging and personally close to his students and staff. A school leader cannot shepherd and lead his school from afar. He must be right there with his people. By doing so, the school leader can gain the trust and allegiance of his students and staff, which are essential for leadership and progress. The activities of a school can be fast-paced, hectic and frenetic, but that is no reason not to know your people.

Michael Fullan once said, "Principals are either overloaded with what they are doing or overloaded with all the things they think they should be doing." Dr. Vicki Wilson, the former assistant superintendent for Henrico County Public Schools, reminded me in my first principalship not to be stuck in my office, behind my title and behind my desk. If I remained in the office, she said, isolated and secluded for any extended periods of time, issue after issue would cleave to me like "fly paper" and paralyze me behind the closed door. I had to be visible, active, engaging and exacting in order to maximize my influence and have a positive impact in the instructional and organizational matters of the school.

Dr. Wilson encouraged me to be intentional and deliberate and to also create opportunities to listen, connect and build as I walked the campus to share with students, staff and stakeholders. "Listen to the voices of your people," she would say, "the students, the parents, the custodial and maintenance staff, cafeteria staff, office staff, guidance staff, instructional staff and other support people." Demonstrate genuine concern and thoughtfulness in what you say and what you do daily. Don't miss a moment to communicate what you believe about students' potential and their importance and value in the work of the school. Regularly convey your thoughts about high achievement for all, more rigorous opportunities for students, and closing the implementation and achievement gaps. Inform your school community, time and again, what you expect in creating a safer and more positive school environment. Iterate how you can generate increased student achievement together and how, as a team, you can support your students in becoming more "future ready." Be authentic and approachable. Walk around the building often and at different times of the day. Visit classrooms and be present in the hallways during transitions, in the lunchroom, on the playground, in staff rooms and the bus loop. Be ubiquitous! Let your staff know who you are and what you stand for. There should be no doubt about priorities and expectations!

Building Relationships

Building positive relationships with your staff is not easy, but it is essential. It will take time, effort, and commitment. You must be intentional and consistent in engaging your staff. As you move throughout the campus, give your staff what John Maxwell calls the "Triple A Treatment" – Attention, Affirmation and Appreciation. Begin by giving your staff your undivided attention. Then, affirm them by highlighting their talents, strengths, importance, and value to the team. And lastly, show your appreciation for them early and often, because what you appreciate, appreciates! It gets better and better and increases in value. Convey an attitude of gratitude, then watch what happens. School relationships can be dramatically enhanced and strengthened when we become encouragers and lifters instead of critics and attackers.

If you want to make a teacher feel extraordinary and valued, then give praise in front of others, especially their students, as well as "one-on-one." Private compliments turned public, instantly increase in impact and significance. Whenever you have the opportunity to publicly praise a staff member, don't let that moment slip by. You can't inspire people to action until you first move them in the heart with hope, sincerity, understanding and compassion. Les Giblin, National Salesman of the Year, stated, "You can't make the other fellow feel important in your presence if you secretly feel that person is a nobody." It is essential that you demonstrate and give respect to all of your people because everyone in your school has value.

In schools, words of encouragement and affirmation matter in the development of building positive relationships. How the school leader communicates to the staff has a tremendous impact on establishing a culture of appreciation, value and support. Effective leaders tend to give far more verbal support and affirmation than criticism, disagreement or ridicule. Less effective leaders and teams tend to use more negative comments.

In their book, *A Passion for Excellence*, Tom Peters and Nancy Austin indicate that the #1 managerial productivity problem in America is quite simply, managers who are out of touch with their people. They don't understand their people. Many educators are highly stressed and emotionally exhausted from providing academic, behavioral, and emotional assistance to their students. So take time to engage and listen. If you desire to understand your people better in order to build connections and a stronger relationship with them, keep in mind John Maxwell's revelations about people:

> People are insecure...give them confidence.
> People want to feel special...sincerely compliment them.
> People desire a better tomorrow...show them hope.
> People need to be understood...listen to them.
> People are selfish...speak to their needs first.
> People get emotionally low...encourage them.
> People want to be associated with success...help them win.

When a school leader understands his people – with their flaws, shortcomings and challenges – and is still able to help them achieve at high levels, he adds value to their lives and makes significant deposits into building a positive relationship with them. Effective leaders are constantly looking for the talents and gifts in others and helping them to develop those gifts.

Here are some additional ideas, my ABCs to building positive relationships:

1. **Appreciate** and applaud teachers for jobs well done via personal notes, cards, emails, letters of commendation and appreciation, during daily announcements, faculty meetings and especially acknowledge them in front of their students.
2. **Acknowledge** and recommend teachers for leadership positions, expanded responsibilities, and special projects. Encourage them to be presenters in school staff development trainings. Build participatory and distributed leadership by encouraging teachers to lead with you and be a part of the decision-making process within the school.
3. **Back** and support teachers as they face and tackle the many tasks and challenges of the work. Teachers need to see their school leaders standing with them as partners and colleagues. Remind teachers how valuable and special they are to the success of their students and the school.
4. **Build** recognition opportunities during faculty meetings, team meetings, special morning breakfasts, and luncheons

honoring staff with small gifts and words of appreciation. Salute the staff for significant years of service (for example: 5, 10, 15, 20, 25…retirement).

5. **Care** for and cherish your staff as individuals and valuable members of the school family. Whenever you have the opportunity to display support and care, I encourage you to never hold back, because every member of your staff is fighting a battle. Demonstrate a willingness and ability to listen and display empathy. Teachers need to know that their leader understands and appreciates their work and recognizes their challenges and frustrations. Show genuine concern when staff members face difficult times in their personal lives such as illness, death in the family, or divorce, etc. Calls, cards, or visits during these critical times will be remembered and will strengthen your relationship with them. Albert Schweitzer said, "Constant kindness can accomplish much. As the sun makes ice melt, kindness causes misunderstanding, mistrust and hostility to evaporate." Show kindness.

6. **Cheer** and celebrate teachers' success when they receive recognition from professional organizations, obtain their post-graduate degrees or certificates, local, state and national awards, promotions, participation on specific committees, or an ABCD Award (A Beyond the Call of Duty Award).

Two powerful lessons in building strong relationships that I have learned over the years are: 1) When you honor people, they will honor you. "When you fail to honor people, they will fail to honor you" (Laozi), and 2) "Three things in human life are important: the first is to be kind; the second is to be kind; and the third is to be kind," (Henry James).

This leads me to a common mistake I want you to avoid that many school leaders make in leading their schools. It is their failure in sharing recognition, hogging the spotlight, and neglecting to extend credit and appreciation to key individuals or the team. This negligence and disregard for the contribution and work of others are significant causes of dissatisfaction within a team. We would be amazed at what we could build and achieve as a school community if we didn't care who got the credit. The bottom line in building relationships isn't how far we advance ourselves, but how far we add value and advance others. So I urge you: Don't pursue glory. Pursue excellence. Invite your team to join the journey with you.

As a school leader, positive relationships with staff and students are directly related to improvement in student achievement, student attendance, student engagement, fewer disruptive behaviors and suspensions, and more positive accolades. So operate out of a strong sense of "it's a love thing." Caring and supporting the school community through strong relationships are extremely important to the success of a school.

"No one can whistle a symphony. It takes a whole orchestra to play it."
— H.E. Luccock

Chapter 5
Teamwork: We are Better Together

The overwhelming truth in leadership is that teamwork is at the heart of all great achievements. Teamwork is what makes schools succeed! A major step in the development and maturity of any school leader is when they realize they cannot do everything alone. It takes leadership and a spirit of community to build effective teams.

"Great things in business are never done by one person; they're done by a team of people." – Steve Jobs

School leaders must decide to trust, include, and empower others to engage in the work and join the journey. My personal evolution and growth as a school principal deepened when I understood that partnering with others would help me do far more than I could do alone. The success and achievement in schools would not increase, soar, or be sustained without strong teamwork and essentially, the staff working in concert. Teamwork, without a doubt, is the lynchpin that sparks and fuels short and long-term successes. You need partners to help you achieve.

"Teamwork is the ability to work together toward a common vision. The ability to direct individual accomplishments toward organizational objectives. It is the fuel that allows common people to attain uncommon results." – Andrew Carnegie

It is clear whenever a school's vision and goals become bolder and larger, there is an intense need for increased teamwork and the coming together as a school family. When school challenges are numerous and compounding, a leader is confronted with two options to consider in moving forward: 1) Give up or abandon the lofty vision and goals or 2) Get help. Courageous and determined leaders choose to get help and build a strong coalition. They tend to be inclusive by expanding the vision and work from "me to we." They expand their influence and reach beyond themselves to others. Effective school leaders believe that when ideas, goals, and the work are shared and embedded in the soul of the school, then energy and momentum will ignite a climate that will birth breakthrough success.

"There is immense power when a group of people with similar interests get together to work toward the same goals." – Idowu Koyenikan

John Maxwell describes the need to work together this way: "When challenges escalate, teamwork must elevate!" If a school is to create positive change, overcome overwhelming obstacles, and tackle tremendous tasks, it can only succeed when operating as a team. When teachers are included in the leadership, they are empowered to lead with you and collaborate. Success comes as a result of people pulling together to achieve common goals.

There must be:

1. **Common Values**: A Shared Vision and Shared Goals
2. **Team Norms**: Do members know what is to be accomplished? And by whom? When? How will it be measured?
3. **Communications are Frequent, Open and Honest**: There is a climate of trust and honesty.

4. **Support is Demonstrated by School Leaders and their Colleagues**
5. **Team Roles Are Clearly Defined**: Who is responsible for what?
6. **Collaborating and Meeting Together** on a Regular Basis
7. **Acceptances of Mutual Accountability** by Individual Team Members and as a Team as a Whole
8. **Encouraging and Respecting a Diversity of Ideas**
9. **Celebrations and Recognitions of Team Achievements**: Success is Imminent

Whenever I think about the importance of teamwork, a funny story that I heard from Dr. Lance Watson brings to light the necessity of working together. He told this story of the bricklayer:

> A man's request for disability was denied pending clarification of that request. The insurance company wrote to him because the basis of his claim was not clear.
>
> Here is what the man wrote back:
>
> *To Whom It May Concern,*
>
> *I am writing a response to your request for additional information in block #3 of the accident report form. I wrote "trying to do the job alone" as the cause of my accident.*
>
> *You said in your letter to me that I should more fully explain and I trust that the following details will be sufficient. I am a bricklayer by trade. On the day of the accident I was working alone on the roof of a six-story building.*

When I completed my work, I discovered that I had approximately 500 pounds of brick left over. Not wanting to waste it, and rather than carry the bricks down by hand, I decided to lower them in a barrel by using the pulley that was attached to the side of the building at the sixth floor.

Securing the rope at ground level, I went up to the roof. I swung the barrel out and then loaded the bricks into it. I then went down to the ground and untied the rope holding it tightly to ensure a slow descent of the brick.

You will note in block #2 of the accident report, it says that I weigh 135 pounds. Due to my surprise, and being jerked off the ground, I lost my presence of mind and did not let go of the rope.

Needless to say, I proceeded at a rather rapid rate up the side of the building. In the vicinity of the third floor, I met the barrel coming down. This explains my broken collar bone.

Slowed only slightly, I continued my rapid ascent up the side of the building until the fingers of my right hand were two knuckles deep in the pulley six floors up. Fortunately, I had the presence of mind to hold on to the rope despite the pain.

At approximately the same time, however, the barrel hit the ground, and the bottom came off and the bricks spilled out. Without the weight of the bricks, the barrel only weighs fifty pounds and I weigh, according to block #2, 135 pounds.

Therefore, as you might imagine, I began a rapid descent down the side of the building and in the vicinity of the third floor. I again met the barrel coming back up.

This accounts for my fractured ankles and the lacerations on my lower body.

The encounter with the barrel slowed me down enough to lessen my injuries when I landed on top of the pile of bricks. I was lying there in pain, and the pain was so intense, I was unable to move. Thinking about my pain, I let go of the rope.

Because my eyes were closed, I did not see the barrel coming back down until it broke both of my legs.

I hope I have furnished enough information to explain how the accident occurred. It occurred because I was trying to do the job alone.

Now, while that might sound absurd, one would be amazed at how many people there are in schools today who are inflicting injury, enduring pain, and suffering hardship because they are trying to do the job alone. Helen Keller once said, "alone we can do so little, but together we can do so much."

Effective and clear teamwork is more than interpersonal relationships. It demands a concerted effort and collaboration toward common goals. If you want to accomplish great things in your school, you must link up and connect with others. One is indeed too small a number to achieve greatness. Why take the journey alone in your school when you can invite and elicit others to join in the work? It is teamwork that gives you the best opportunity to turn your school vision into reality.

"Because in any organization we are better together! When there is love, teamwork and collaboration, wonderful things can be achieved." - Mattie Stepanek

"Teamwork makes the dream work!"
— John Maxwell

Chapter 6
Distributive Leadership: Lead with Me

As I reflect upon my leadership experiences at Virginia Randolph Community High School, Henrico High School, and in Mooresville Graded School District, the importance of teamwork and building collective capacity through distributive leadership were essential. As a school and district organization, we could only facilitate increased student achievement once we behaved as a unit, as a team. I knew there was tremendous, transformative power in collective effort and synergy.

As principal, I realized that I was not the only leader in the school. Teachers, assistant principals, parents, students, and community members each had a key role in making decisions that impacted student performances. The message I wanted to convey was "lead with me." I needed their help, their hand, their heart, and their expertise in advancing our school agenda. I needed their input, their ideas, their support, their energy, and their corporate effort more than ever.

In the summer of 2002, Henrico High School was the only high school in Henrico County Public Schools that was not "fully accredited," as measured by the Virginia Standards of Learning. There were climate issues, pockets of low expectations for students, and a lack of schoolwide focus. The Henrico High School staff was a great staff, full of talented and extraordinary teachers, but was not operating as a cohesive community with a laser-like focus. A number of staff members did not believe, nor behaved, like our students could learn and achieve at high levels. We struggled with widespread low student achievement results in one or more subjects and grade levels. We battled with too many students with special needs and low socio-economic students not meeting state achievement standards. However, with strong central office support, we were able to move forward with confidence to facilitate the much needed school reform.

With the challenges before us, I knew we could achieve far more together. Henrico High School could not climb this enormous mountain divided or fragmented. We had to pull together for the sake of our students! We had to convince the adults in the building that it was up to us to be the change that we sought. It was imperative that we strived together to reach our goals. It was in our collective hands. It was distributive leadership and teamwork that gave us the best opportunity to turn this vision into reality.

Through research of the school's data and numerous conversations with the administrative team, teacher leaders, the entire staff, parents, students, and community leaders, it was determined that we needed a clear **vision** of what we wanted Henrico High School to become. We needed a collective effort, commitment, clear communications and a strong sense of accountability.

We asked teachers who taught the same content area or grade level to work more collaboratively in planning lessons and developing common assessments. We urged them to commit to the idea of one response of extra time and extra instruction when students struggled and/or failed. We requested for them to increase their communication with their parents. We implored them to share ideas, best practices and resources, offer support, organize professional development training and hold each other accountable to the work, to department targets, and to school goals.

As we crafted the slogan and image of "Going Over the Top," it was essential that we gave our students and staff the mental picture of what we expected to achieve as a school family. We also wanted to give our school community an affirmative reputation to uphold and a target to hit. In every classroom, we posted our school goals and a picture of a pole vaulter going over the bar. Everyone knew the mission was possible and it was reiterated at every meeting (faculty, department, leadership, student assembly, business partnership meeting, and PTA meeting). It was important for us to stay on message and keep the main thing, the main thing!

From the beginning, we understood the necessity, not only to strengthen the existing leadership team, but to enlist the talents and positive energies of other committed teacher leaders on campus. There were a number of teachers who were anxious and hungry to serve at a higher level of contribution and leadership. Through additional responsibilities, increased recognition, and the opportunity for advancements, we were able to strengthen and extend our leadership reach by "deputizing" teacher leaders and soliciting their support. Many tasks in the school were distributed and facilitated through committees and teams.

We looked closely at our department chair leadership positions. We wanted individuals who exhibited a deep passion for teaching and learning, who cared about students, facilitated outstanding student results, displayed a history of working collaboratively with people, and were optimistic about the hard work ahead. In some cases, we also established co-chairs to share the responsibilities of the team recognizing that two heads are better than one. We also wanted to be proactive about the reality of leadership succession — when a department chair retires or transfers. We wanted to be prepared and to sustain the momentum, cohesiveness and flow within the department. We expanded the number of administrative aide positions (full-time teachers who had a duty period with some administrative assignments included). The district also included two new positions, an administrative intern and a new teacher instructional coach. The administrative intern was an identified teacher pursuing their administrative degree or a teacher with an administrative degree. This position was a great opportunity for promising administrative leaders to gain extraordinary leadership experiences in the work, like a trial run. It was similar to having an additional administrator. Principals and assistant principals were handed this gift, and we afforded this budding leader the exposure, support and direction while they were preparing for an administrative position. We examined the leadership on school committees and made some changes which included the creation of new committees to address specific building level needs.

Creating an environment of inclusion, leadership opportunities and encouragement helped transform people's lives and our school. "It is time," Moller and Pankake write, "for principals to intentionally move from serving as the director of school actions to being a coach for teacher leaders."

We recognized the need to invest more in the professional and instructional growth of our administrative and teacher leaders. We made a concerted effort to engage and empower them in their leadership roles and responsibilities. No longer would we expect leaders to operate as mere dispensers of information in meetings; instead, they would operate as problem-solvers, facilitators and leaders with a stronger sense of responsibility to achieve the goals of the school. We realized that no matter what programs we introduced, our most important work and investment were to improve the leaders in our school. We elevated the importance and focus in professional development training. Our effort was aimed at equipping our leaders in their growth in instructional and leadership matters. We met with the faculty, departments, key school leaders and district content area specialists to identify needs and the appropriate training critical for our school in growing forward. We met, discussed, and planned summer institutes, opening week training, and monthly ongoing training. Professional training was vital in re-energizing the staff; building individual and team confidence; developing leadership capacity among key teacher leaders; improving our school-wide delivery of instruction to students; and preparing for leadership succession. Each assistant principal worked closely with their respective departments in creating its professional learning plan. The proposal was based on department, content area and individual teacher needs. The educational specialists were also key in providing guidance, expertise and resources in strengthening this plan.

Our students could not win without our collective effort. Everyone had to focus and work for the greater good of the school and this noble cause. Our school reform depended upon this shared leadership and commitment. The team became far greater than any one individual. As the new principal, I found myself asking three things: 1) What do we need to do to preserve and honor the leaders before me? 2) What do we need to do in order to provide a sense of continuity of the past? and 3) What do we need to change to send a clear signal that this is a new day and we are going in a new direction toward a more excellent way?

We kicked off our efforts to build synergy and traction at the school's opening meeting when staff reported. PTA officers, central office administration, business leaders, school board members, and the community at-large were all invited to attend the meeting. We gave every person attending a two-foot green or gold (school colors) thread of yarn. Located at the center of the room was an empty "Little Red Wagon," shiny and new. Hidden under a blanket near the wagon were ten large landscape bricks, each labeled, representing a school-wide challenge:

1. Full Accreditation
2. Extra Help Opportunities

3. Staff Development Training
4. Safe and Orderly Environment
5. Literacy Plan
6. Improved Student Attendance
7. Increased Graduation Rate
8. Technology
9. Classroom Management
10. Teamwork

I shared with the stakeholders that each initiative needed a corporate "All In" effort as I dropped each brick in the wagon with a loud "boom!" I took my green yarn and tied it to the handle of the little red wagon and attempted to pull the wagon forward. Alone, I could not move the wagon with such a heavy load; however, collectively, I knew that we were better and stronger together. I asked everyone in the school family to tie their yarn to the handle. Over 170 stakeholders tied their yarn to the handle that morning and we were able to move the wagon with ease. Victory is always within our reach when we pull together!

The point of this illustration was to invite all stakeholders to join us on this journey together. It was an engaging way to ask for their commitment in shouldering the responsibilities and in sharing in the leadership. We realized we could not do the work in isolation or in silos. It would require all of us in a community effort to move our school in the right direction.

Exceptional student results occur when the extraordinary challenges that our students face are met with an even greater level of adult leadership commitment, caring and competence. When the dedicated, focused adult school community works collaboratively together, outstanding student outcomes will occur. The concept "lead with me" was crystal clear. Distributive leadership and teamwork were essential in transforming our school and generating the desired student results.

As a school, we also made a conscientious decision to focus on improving "teaching and learning." Each content department was challenged to develop an improvement plan which became its roadmap to academic victory. The department's job was to determine how best to teach the curriculum, use the available resources, create effective assessments, collaborate, and provide instructional interventions. The assistant principals and department chairs provided leadership, ensuring an effective and thoughtful plan. We wanted to make certain that each plan was inclusive, detailed, comprehensive and supported by everyone within the department. There were times the plans were returned for further review. We requested the departments to have a laser-like focus on student achievement and to develop specific strategies to facilitate improvement. The plans were expected to display clarity, convey a "sense of urgency," and mutual accountability. The feedback provided by the administration led to a stronger blueprint for student success. Each department was expected to do everything possible to increase student achievement to "full accreditation."

Daily classroom observations were expected and played a central role in our school achievement. The real work of "teaching and learning" takes place in the classroom. Our success as a school rested on what was happening in those classrooms. So, it was incumbent upon the leadership team to help teachers apply effective pedagogy in the delivery of instruction. The administrative team, department chairs and central office administrators increased visibility, support, and intervention in an effort to increase the quality of the learning experiences for our students. We could only succeed through on-going staff development, courageous conversations, and honest feedback with the focus always on the results. Lesson plans in alignment with the state standards, teaching bell to bell, incorporating differentiation, the use of instructional technology, common assessment results, and intervention logs were all monitored in the spirit of improving student achievement. These accountability measures revealed the "heart" of our schoolwide commitment and generated momentum. Our determined and resolute pursuit encouraged our students and staff to make exceptional gains.

Distributive leadership is a love thing! It is about the mobilization of individuals, departments, and teams within the schools or district where no single person holds all the power all of the time. Leadership is shared and roles are flexible. Individuals and teams are empowered to take initiative and share in the responsibility, plan and operation of the school community. It is our moral obligation to provide a high quality education, regardless of students' abilities, backgrounds or family incomes. We should extend reach, become more inclusive, and tap into the extraordinary talents and strengths within our students and our school's community. It is a love thing because everyone has the potential and opportunity to lead in their area of interest and strength to make significant contributions to the overall success of the school or district.

"Great teachers and administrators are like candles — they light the way for others."
— Mustafa Kemal Ataturk

Chapter 7
The Power of Instructional Delivery

The power of instructional delivery is a love thing! Love and care originate and sprout from deep within the instructional leader's heart, with the payoff of empowering and lifting students. Effective and thoughtful instruction is one of the greatest acts of love that can influence students and change their lives forever. It has the reach and capacity to touch eternity, especially when leaders approach their students and their work with an eternal and timeless perspective. Nelson Mandela once said, "education is the most powerful weapon which can be used to change the world." I am a passionate believer that teaching is definitely a love thing and must be approached and delivered with a positive and eternal mindset.

Effective instruction is ignited when teachers and instructional leaders believe wholeheartedly in their students' abilities and learning potential, and then behave in alignment with that deep, fundamental belief. Every interaction, spoken word of affirmation, encouragement, act of kindness and compassion from a competent, caring educator has the power to transform lives by stirring up the gifts within their students and inspiring rich possibilities for a productive future.

Great teachers and leaders understand, without a doubt, that what they do in the classroom matters! What they say matters and impacts the lives of their students. Great school leaders take great ownership and pride in their work and in the achievements of their students. They view themselves as responsible for the teaching, learning and success of their students. They are, in Napoleon's words, "merchants of hope!" They deeply understand that their influence, leverage, and impact rest within how they behave when their students cross the threshold of the classroom door. That is where the nurturance, high expectations and love join together to make a difference. Caring and competent instructional leaders believe, regardless of their students' zip codes, community issues or family dynamics, what they do matters and can change a student's achievement, trajectory and outlook!

My growth as a teacher and as an instructional leader was greatly influenced and impacted by a number of leadership heroes from Richmond Public Schools and Henrico County Public Schools: Dr. Beverly Braxton, Dr. Roberta Caston, Dr. Wilbert Jenkins, Dr. Vicki Wilson, Dr. Harold Lawson, and Dr. Mark Edwards. They deposited their time and a treasure chest of knowledge, expertise and insights into my professional growth. They poured encouragement, guidance and support that afforded me extraordinary opportunities to grow and to find my footing as a school leader. Because of their ongoing mentoring and coaching, my instructional leadership accelerated.

As I prepared in the "waiting room" for administrative leadership positions, the demand for effective instructional leaders grew. I knew I had to invest more time and energy into my professional development to be ready to lead a school and create positive change. I became more intentional and relentless in reading books and articles on instructional leadership, school improvement, and the best practices in the delivery of instruction. Educational authors and researchers such as Madeline Hunter, Ron Edmonds, Larry Lezotte, Robert Marzano, Rick and Betsy Dufour, Michael Fullan, Benjamin Bloom, John Maxwell, Todd Whitaker, John Hattie, Harry Wong, Fred Jones, Pedro Noguera, Linda Darling-Hammond, to name just a few, heavily impacted my thinking and progress.

I also frequently visited the Virginia Department of Education's website for updates, ideas, resources and strategies on school improvement. I was hungry and determined to improve so I could serve more effectively and productively. I made it a priority to attend workshops and webinars. Each summer, I attended national conferences such as the *SREB High Schools That Work Conference*, the *International Baccalaureate Conference*, the *National Association of Secondary School Principals Conference* (NASSP) or the *ASCD Summer Conference*.

Dr. Caston, my assistant principal at Henderson Middle School in Richmond, Virginia, was a huge supporter and advocate when I was a budding teacher. She would call me into her office and present me with "in basket" leadership learning opportunities. She shared some of the challenges, demands and responsibilities of the day that landed on her desk. She often asked, "Bill, how would you handle this? What do you think about this? What steps or course of action would you take to resolve this situation? What questions would you ask? How would you provide guidance and support to this teacher, this department, this student or this parent?"

Do you wish to evolve as a leader? Then begin by laying a foundation of humility and preparation. I believe respect, humility and a genuine receptiveness to guidance are key to leadership success because it places you in the proper spirit and posture of learning with an open heart and mind. Listening and learning from proven practitioners and school experts about the latest evidence-based strategies, their successes, their mountaintop and valley experiences, and even their failures deepened my commitment and preparation for expanded school leadership. The more I grew, the more I would be able to share and build on fresh, new ideas, approaches and proven practices to someday lead a school.

Impacting Instruction

Working in schools and studying evidence-based pedagogy and best instructional practices have taught me that there is a methodology to effective teaching. When planning or implementing a lesson, there are specific components I have observed which are essential to engaging and enhancing student learning. Teachers need to have a foundation of content knowledge and instructional skills to effectively increase student achievement. The following components are critical:

1) A deep and comprehensive understanding of the curriculum content to be taught
2) To engage in thoughtful planning in the designing of lessons that are tightly aligned with state standards in both content and in the level of cognition to meet the needs of your students

3) To strategically use instructional resources and support materials to make learning inviting, relevant and fun
4) To effectively present and deliver instruction in a manner that meets students at their level of interest and engagement and breathes life, purpose and meaning into a lesson
5) To incorporate proficient and valid classroom management strategies
6) To exhibit warm, kind and welcoming humanistic qualities with the sole purpose of connecting with students, knowing them as individuals, and demonstrating a strong sense of caring and commitment to meet students at their instructional point of need

These core components of Madeline Hunter's "Total Teaching Act" and the variations that followed her work greatly influenced my understanding and approach of what effective teaching looks like and how I can competently and consistently assist and guide teachers in their instructional work to increase student achievement.

The Teacher Factor Matters (Humanistic Qualities)
The Teacher Factor pales all others! The classroom teacher is by far the most important factor and catalyst in determining the academic success of students. Research identifies teacher quality as the most influential and effective school-related factor impacting student achievement. As Jennifer King Rice notes, "All significant accomplishments in the classroom happen because of the teacher's human qualities connecting, inspiring, pushing, lifting and encouraging their students."

Mark Twain once said, *"When dealing with people, remember you are not dealing with creatures of logic, but creatures of emotion."* As educators, this saying conveys that the way to our students' heads and to their academic performance is through the heart. We cannot overlook the significance and value of bonding and relating with students. Connecting and relating with students starts in the heart and are fundamental in creating positive relationships and a learning environment which lay the groundwork for learning.

As leaders, we should be guided by the importance of connecting and building positive relationships with our students and treating them as valued individuals, deserving of respect, kindness and fairness. Respect, kindness and fairness are powerful influencers and motivators, but they must be substantive and real in the eyes of students in order for them to perform at high levels. When teachers fill their classrooms with kindness and genuine concern, authentic praise, honest, constructive and encouraging feedback and recognition of their students' backgrounds and cultures, the odds of capturing a student's heart is greatly enhanced. When students have positive interactions with their teacher and feel valued and supported, they will become more focused and engaged in learning. Important messages conveyed by caring and compassionate teachers are:

"You are important to me!"

"I believe in you!"

"I trust in you."

"You will achieve!"

"I am here to help you succeed!"

"In this class, you are listened to, cared for, and valued!"

I believe that teachers are the most prominent and dynamic resource in the classroom. The quality and effectiveness of teaching and learning start with the teacher's **love** for their students, their love for learning, and their commitment and devotion to their students' success.

When teachers are motivated by a strong respect for their students and a deep commitment to meeting their unique needs, they create rich, engaging learning experiences that foster growth.

"The single greatest effect on student achievement is not race. It is not poverty. It is the effectiveness of the teacher." – Harry Wong

Knowledge of Content Matters
Teachers are expected to have a deep and proficient understanding of the body of knowledge to be taught. Possessing this knowledge or

passionately pursuing this knowledge is a love thing! Effective teaching not only involves fully understanding the curriculum content to be taught, but also how to deliver the knowledge in real life applications that are sensitive to their students' backgrounds. It is clear-cut and obvious to me that teachers must wholly understand the subject matter they are teaching in order to yield greater student results.

Content is the heart of the teaching profession! It is the written curriculum, the planned course of study, and respective experiences that are expected to be taught to students and subsequently, achieved. Teaching is taking students from a space of not knowing to a place of knowing, proficiency and confidence. It is working diligently to lead students in learning new things and transferring that learning to new situations. The result of effective instructional delivery is to increase students' essential knowledge and understanding, to problem solve, to ask questions, to discuss, and ultimately, to elevate and enrich students' lives. You cannot teach what you do not know. You cannot lead or effectively guide students where you have not been or experienced. Thus, knowledge of the subject matter is most critical.

Capable and well informed teachers can fully explain, instruct, inspire, and model more effectively to their students as a result of their thorough grasp and understanding of the subject matter. William A. Ward once said, "The mediocre teacher tells; the good teacher explains; the superior teacher demonstrates; but the great teacher inspires." He went on to further say, "Teaching is more than imparting knowledge; it is inspiring change." Learning is more than absorbing facts; it is acquiring in-depth understanding and having the ability to transfer and apply knowledge and understanding to new situations. It is preparing students to become "future ready" with a real world perspective.

Instructional Planning Matters

Devising instructional lesson plans is a love thing! Lesson planning is the effective teacher's blueprint and guide for learning and teaching. It is the roadmap of what students are expected to learn, how the learning will be achieved, and how the learning will be assessed at the end of the lesson. The teacher's lesson plan is the step-by-step, thoughtful, detailed game plan that provides the structure and framework for the delivery of ideas, decisions, actions and experiences toward essential learning.

My wife, Pamela, was a high school special education teacher and department chair. In her retirement, she launched a career as a **wedding coordinator.** The meticulous planning skills once used to facilitate the achievement and success of her students and department were then used to organize a loving couple's special day of bliss and joy. A **building contractor**, before erecting a house or any edifice, prepares very detailed plans and blueprints. A **head football coach**, on game day, takes the field with his team with a strategic game plan designed for victory. **Military commanders**, in preparation for battle, prepare very analytical plans with contingencies and alternate plans before going into a fierce fight. A **gourmet chef**, in any prominent fine dining restaurant, has a plan for preparing exquisite cuisines with a variety of delicious entrees and meals. An **airplane pilot** has flight plans to prepare and review before heading down the runway and taking off into the "friendly skies" to ensure safe travel and a smooth landing at a scheduled destination. As such, **classroom teachers** must very well have thoughtful and deliberate plans to lead their students to achievement and academic victory. Generally, teachers make over a thousand instructional decisions a day. So the quality of these decisions is crucial in engaging and leading students to increased participation and success.

Planning a lesson reveals the collaboration of the art and science of instruction when capturing students' hearts and interests. The art in lesson planning involves the personality of the teacher, the intuitive nature, the style, the passion, the creative side, the imagination, voice and the intensity of the teacher. The science part of planning constitutes the application of evidence-based practices, strategies and pedagogy. The skillful teacher needs both art and science in the construction of effective lesson planning and in the delivery of effective instruction to maximize student learning.

Whenever I visited and observed classrooms where there were instructional concerns, such as low student academic performance results and widespread student disengagement and disruption, taking a closer look into the teachers' lesson plans was necessary and imperative. A deeper dive into the planning allows leadership the opportunity to sit down with teachers and ask reflective and clarifying questions in an effort to guide teachers in the improvement of their instructional decisions and to provide targeted intervention and support.

Lesson plans reveal the level of expectations teachers have of their students' learning capacity. Whether high or low, teacher decisions expose the degree of commitment they are willing to exert in meeting the varied learning needs of their students. The plans also communicate whether they possess an unwavering belief that every student has the ability to learn at higher levels.

Lesson plans also show how responsive teachers are to their students' circumstances, their backgrounds and their cultures. Does the teacher's **beliefs, views, perspectives** and **will** serve in the best interest of their students? Does the teacher project an asset growth mindset or does the teacher's low expectations, biases and temperament hinder student progress? Is the teacher dedicated and committed to the progress of each learner to meet and exceed state standards, regardless of their zip code or demographics? The level of their conviction and belief system are undoubtedly embedded in every decision outlined in their lesson plans.

Lesson plans also divulge the depth of the teacher's insight into how students learn; their awareness of their students' learning styles and needs; and how the teacher plans to respond to those demands. Lesson planning is truly a love thing and it clearly publishes the beliefs, values, and mindset of teachers. Therefore, as we help teachers grow in this process, frequent examinations of lesson plans by the administration is necessary to analyze the quality and depth of the plans!

Moreover, it is also extremely important for administrators to be a part of the lesson planning with individual teachers or cluster/grade level teachers as they plan. This practice of leading and guiding the focus is of great value in building instructional leadership capacity and improving the instructional decisions of teachers with the ultimate goal of increasing student success. Listening carefully to teachers through this planning process – their thoughts, ideas, and strategies – as they plan learning experiences for their students is critical. During this time, the administrator is able to ask a number of reflective, probing and clarifying questions in guiding teachers in elevating their instructional decisions as they prepare quality lesson plans. Of course, to make the greatest impact in this collaboration, this time together must be conducted and grounded in a climate of trust and mutual respect. It must also possess a willingness to add value and to demonstrate genuine care about the instructional growth of the teacher and their students' academic success.

Asking the right instructional questions can make a tremendous difference in the quality of the teachers' instructional decision making. Administrators' questions can be helpful in stretching teachers in meeting their students' needs.

Here are some instructional questions for consideration:

1. How do you know your learning activities are aligned with the state standards?
2. What state or district resources are you using in your planning? How are they helpful to you?
3. Upon students entering the classroom, how will you immediately engage them in learning?
4. What is the learning target for today?
5. What do you want students to achieve by the end of the lesson?
6. How will you provide clarity so students will know exactly what is expected of them?
7. How will you activate prior student knowledge to link today's lesson with previous learning?
8. How will you spark and capture student attention and convince them to proceed at the start of the lesson?
9. What instructional activities, resources and materials will you use in your lesson to lead students to mastery?
10. How will you teach to the eye? Give examples.
11. Describe what your direct instruction, guided practice and independent practices will look like in the lesson?
12. How will you help students make real life connections? How will you build relevancy and meaning in the lesson?

13. Describe ways you demonstrate and ensure culturally responsive teaching practices in your lessons.
14. Describe the population of your classes.
15. Describe how you will monitor learning throughout the lesson.
16. What does it look like when you check for understanding?
17. How often will you check for understanding and what methods will you use?
18. How will you differentiate your instruction to meet the varied needs of your students? What will it look like?
19. Are your planned learning experiences timed or chunked in short, engaging intervals?
20. How do you convey a sense of urgency and with-it-ness in your lesson?
21. What will rigor and higher order questioning and thinking look like in this lesson? Give examples.
22. Are your questions prepared in advance?
23. Are you familiar with Bloom's Question Stems and Bloom's Taxonomy Circles?
24. Are students frequently asked to justify their answer(s)? To explain in their own words? To summarize what they learned? To explain how they arrived at their answer(s)? To elaborate on their answer(s)? To give examples or illustrations? Do they agree? Disagree? Explain why?
25. Are you providing opportunities for student discussions in small groups or with a partner (think-pair-share)?
26. Describe how you plan to increase student interaction and student ownership of their learning.
27. How are you integrating literacy in your lesson? Describe how you are supporting reading, writing, and speaking.
28. How will you provide extra help opportunities for struggling students as a result of student data? How and when will it be provided?
29. What will you do differently to ensure a different result?
30. What will the co-teaching instructional model look like in your inclusion classroom?
31. Describe the collaboration work with your co-teacher? What does it look like?
32. Describe how you plan to meet your Student With Disability (SWD) needs?

33. Describe how you plan to meet the needs of your English Language Learner (ELL) students?
34. How do you plan to end your lesson? What will the closure set look like? Are students actively involved? How will you get them actively involved?
35. How will you know that students have mastered the objectives?
36. What will the closing assessment look like? What should the students be able to do or achieve by the end of the lesson to exhibit mastery?
37. How will students demonstrate learning?
38. How will you adjust tomorrow's lesson in light of today's student results?
39. How will you provide support for students who are having difficulty with today's lesson? What will you do differently to ensure their success?

These questions are not intended to intimidate the teacher and all of them are not necessarily used when assisting with planning. The questions are designed to guide teachers in becoming more proactive, thoughtful, intentional, fixed, focused and responsive in addressing the multiple instructional needs of their students and to create quality lesson plans.

Years of experience and constant delving into the latest instructional research have shown me that student achievement is directly related to and impacted by teachers' thoughtful planning and the quality of their decisions. Therefore, effective instructional leadership is a love thing. Love and care are found within the questions, feedback, guidance and support given to teachers in the effort to lead them in their improved instructional decisions for their lesson planning.

Instructional Resources Matter
Creating and integrating instructional resources and materials is a love thing! A significant component in the delivery of instruction is the teacher's incorporation of instructional resources and materials in their lessons with the purpose of engaging and lifting students. These valuable instructional resources and materials are critical in helping intended learning experiences come alive with meaning, excitement,

clarity and focus. In today's fluid learning environment of both in-person learning and online classrooms, teachers must ensure that the instructional resources and materials meet the content and cognitive level(s) as written within state standards and also operate through the acute lens of a diverse community. Therefore, these "tools for teaching" must be carefully and thoughtfully selected and planned with students' needs, styles and backgrounds in mind in order to spark and promote maximum student engagement and student learning.

Instructional resources and materials are invaluable in lessons because they add academic significance, richness and energy to capture students' attention then hold their interest and engagement in the classroom lesson. Student learning is strengthened when the planned learning experiences include multi-sensory and multi-modality approaches (visual, auditory, kinesthetic, and tactile) in the instructional delivery. Every teacher needs to include different spices and ingredients of resources and materials to enrich their lessons because students learn differently and require different stimuli and experiences to engage them and lead them to success.

Many students are strong **auditory listeners**. They learn more effectively by listening. These students comprehend facts and concepts by listening closely and intently to lectures, group discussions, oral presentations, podcasts, storytelling, voice recordings, short songs, and debates, to name a few. *Visual learners*, on the other hand, rely heavily on the optical, observable aspects of learning. They absorb, understand, remember and process things more keenly by sight. With the use of pictures, illustrations, videos, diagrams, charts, maps, etc., learning is more engaging and effective for them. The ***kinesthetic learner*** grasps, digests, retains and experiences learning best by doing, touching, constructing and moving. Deep learning occurs for them through physical activities, hands-on experiences, drawing and role playing.

All students learn through a combination of different learning styles (seeing, hearing and doing), but one style may be more compelling and dominant. Thus, the clear and profound message to all teachers is to take the needed time to assess, investigate and determine the distinct learning styles and needs of students to plan accordingly with varied, targeted and specific learning experiences to meet the diverse instructional needs of their students.

Teacher-Made Resources and Materials Matter
Some classroom resources are created by the teacher to make lessons more interesting, easier, exciting, engaging and targeted to support students' learning in the instructional process. These resources are materials such as handouts, teacher-made quizzes, tests, foldables, word walls, hands-on materials, videos, presentations, and more. With these resources and materials, students have the opportunity to see, hear and feel the teacher-made resources which enhance learning.

Through *printed materials* such as textbooks, workbooks, manuals, documents, charts, tables, maps, graphic organizers, Venn diagrams, illustrations, photographs, posters, whiteboards, index cards, and others, the teacher can boost student lessons and increase student learning.

Technology through digital devices and multimedia tools are tremendously important today and are beneficial in advancing student learning. Technology is drastically transforming the landscape and learning environment of instructional delivery in and outside of the classroom. It is a dynamic, fluid resource that teachers can use at their discretion and is an essential part of today's education system.

This digital conversion represents a cultural shift in our schools. The COVID-19 Pandemic accelerated the demand and use of digital devices and programs to serve our students in remote learning. The internet, with its viewing and retrieval of information, is easily accessible in many localities but is scarce and deficient in others. This broadband disparity must be corrected and improved if our schools are to serve in a more comprehensive and convenient manner for all of our students.

Because of technology, teachers and students no longer are limited to information found in textbooks and printed materials and also are not limited in time. The integration of technology in education with devices such as computers, laptops, Chromebooks, Zoom, clicker technology, Wi-Fi, Google collaboration tools, calculators, videos, PowerPoint presentations, movie clips, social media, podcasts, learner-created videos, recordings, YouTube videos, digital instructional programs, AI and more, is impacting the teaching and learning processes in profound and extraordinary ways.

Technology is making teaching and learning more meaningful, accessible, and fun in preparing students to become "future ready" with the ability to compete and thrive in post-secondary training and industries. These digital learning tools will not only strengthen and enhance students' learning experiences, but will also save teachers valuable instructional time by reducing the amount of time spent on administrative tasks. Students will also have the opportunity to exhibit ownership of their learning with technology by enabling them to track and monitor their academic progress. When students own and take greater responsibility in their learning, they have a higher motivation to learn and achieve stronger academic performance in school *("Ownership of Learning")*.

Additionally, Artificial Intelligence (AI) is impacting education today and we need to understand its impact and vast potential. Teachers and school districts have been debating and wrestling with how to respond to this emerging and surging technology because ultimately, it will transform the way we work, learn and communicate. The major question in our schools is how can AI advance teaching and learning. From personalized lessons to virtual tutors, AI is making education more engaging, accessible and smarter. It helps teachers modify and enhance lessons to meet the varied needs of students, allowing students' learning to be more interactive and engaging. AI tools, such as chatbots and adaptive learning systems, offer instant feedback, making the learning process more connected and effective. Education today cannot avoid AI but is rather encouraged to explore and harness the strengths and benefits of this revolutionary and innovative technology to ensure it is used ethically, equitably and safely.

As described above, instructional resources and materials come in a wide assortment, and each has a capacity and purpose to support and influence student learning. Instructional learning materials and resources are crucial in teaching and learning when presented thoughtfully and strategically because they provide planned sensory experiences to increase student engagement and achievement.

Instructional Delivery Matters
Instructional delivery is a powerful love thing! This is where the fire of learning is ignited and fueled by a caring, loving and knowledgeable educator. Effective teaching saturates the heart, mind and spirit of caring teachers with the sole purpose of inviting and persuading young people to join the journey of discovery and learning. Effective teaching involves the rich interaction among the students, the teacher, the content and the instructional resources working collectively to fill the classroom with excitement, curiosity, confidence, achievement and the possibility of a more promising future.

As teachers work to increase student achievement, they must possess an acute understanding of "how they teach matters!" How they organize their classroom matters! How they approach and plan learning experiences matters! How they connect and relate to students matters!

In order to have a dynamic and influential impact in the classroom, skillful teachers consistently apply evidence-based instructional pedagogy. It is imperative that teachers incorporate the teaching strategies that have been proven to work effectively with diverse learners. Yes, as stated earlier, how we teach matters! When teachers routinely incorporate powerful pedagogical practices in the classroom, these strategies result in greater student engagement and increased student outcomes.

There are a number of focused areas in my classrooms that observation looks for, but the #1 indicator and barometer of a teacher's effectiveness in instructional delivery is ***student engagement***. I constantly take quick visual scans of the classroom during my visit to observe the degree of active involvement of students with their teacher. I focus on what students are doing and their level of engagement with the teacher, the content being presented, and the instructional resource(s). I observe if students are leaning into the lesson with interest, are absorbed, or fascinated. Are they exhibiting the proper posture for learning — vertical and upright? Are they tracking the speaker and maintaining eye contact? Are they alert, sitting on "go"?

I assess whether students are displaying an energy and connection through their responses, comments, restatements, reflections, questions, explanations, examples, illustrations or ideas. I examine whether students are demonstrating an eagerness and a willingness to participate and proceed in the planned learning experiences. Are they taking it all in, consuming, comprehending, sharing, discussing or disagreeing? When instruction captures students' attention and touches their heart, learning deepens and is accelerated.

The Beginning of Class
In any classroom, the first five to ten minutes of the lesson are extremely important in launching and advancing the instructional lesson. This is the learning take-off and springboard! The Anticipatory Set, as Madeline Hunter composed and described years ago, is crucial in setting the stage for learning by providing the "hook." It's the attraction, the instructional persuasion, that captures students' attention, ignites their interest, and inspires them to proceed. It can also provide an opportunity for an instructional review of previous learning to connect that learning experience to today's instructional lesson.

The Anticipatory Set places students in a position of readiness and preparation. This planned activity is designed to quickly get students involved in the lesson and to fully engage them in the targeted learning experiences to come. During the introduction, teachers make clear what students are expected to learn, do and achieve by the end of the lesson. This teacher's clarity is vital! John Hattie's research in 2009 informs us that when teachers are clear in their expectations and instruction, students learn more. According to Hattie, teacher clarity is one of the most potent influences on student achievement. During this instructional entrance, teachers are intentional and clear in informing students of the planned learning experiences, activities and resources that will be used to lead them to this fresh, new learning and how they will be measured and assessed to determine if they have mastered the learning.

This admittance into learning, often begins with a **Do Now, a Warm-Up or a Bellringer,** whatever you choose to call it. Each is used as a management and instructional tool created to engage students immediately upon their arrival into the classroom. When students enter the classroom, the teacher's clear purpose is to maximize time on-task by getting students immediately involved in the lesson. This curbs any idle, unproductive or ineffectual behavior which would prevent students from participating cognitively and behaviorally in the warm-up.

As stated by Harry Wong, "no learning occurs when students are idled, distracted, off task or when the teacher is disciplining them. Learning takes place when students are engaged, involved and working." So my strong recommendation to every teacher at the start of each lesson is to get their students in the habit of being engaged upon entering the classroom. I urge teachers to give deep and intense thought to establishing the daily operation of instructional warm-ups in the classroom learning environment.

Here are a few helpful examples of warm-ups that can be used to engage students immediately upon their arrival to the classroom: posted questions, a quick quiz, a quick write, a problem, a quote, an illustration, a drawing, a photo, a short video, a song, a short vocabulary list, or a word chain.

Direct Instruction
In direct instruction, teachers are directing the instructional delivery and process toward their students. They are not only teaching their students the things they need to learn, but are also showing them how to master concepts they must be able to do for themselves. Direct instruction is an evidence-based teaching strategy led by a competent and caring teacher who is equipped with a deep understanding of the subject matter to be taught and a strong knowledge of their students' strengths and learning needs. These skillful teachers are keenly aware of their students' abilities, interests and background and are capable of connecting with and involving their students because of their attention and knowledge. This teacher-led, straightforward experience occurs when the teacher stands and delivers before their students with energy and passion. The teacher presents instructional material and information in an

organized and inviting step-by-step manner and at the students' correct level of interest and difficulty.

The most used direct instruction method is the classroom lecture. This is probably the clearest and most definitive illustration of direct instruction and the most common teaching technique in the teachers' instructional arsenal. During direct instruction, the teacher is able to use their creativity and inventiveness to capture student attention and engage them with intriguing and interesting information, fascinating and fun facts, captivating and compelling content, exciting and explicit explanations, riveting and remarkable recounts and reports, accurate and astonishing accounts, and startling and sensational statements. To juice up and excite the instructional delivery and moment even more, add a touch of storytelling for relevancy, additional clarity and connection!

In recent years, direct instruction has been under fire and has received negative feedback, especially when there is an overreliance on "teacher talk" in the classroom. The culprit is when teachers implement a heavy, insensitive dose of lecture, often too long and monotonous, which causes students to quickly grow bored, inattentive and to zone out. A remedy to this mundane and dull experience is found when learning activities (i.e. teacher talks) are chunked into small, bite-size instructional intervals, which are interactive and influenced by the teacher's knowledge of their students' instructional needs. When there is a mixture and fusion of teacher modeling, demonstrations, labs, displaying of pictures, illustrations and videos, hands-on experiences and opportunities for students to discuss, look for similarities and differences, cause and effect, ask questions and collaborate with their partners and in groups, student achievement is greatly enhanced and increased.

Guided Practice
Guided practice is a significant part of the planned lesson where students become more actively involved in their learning. After the direct instructional learning experiences, the teacher gradually turns over the learning reins to the students, but remains vigilant alongside and resolute to provide support and assistance to students as needed, leading them to increased learning. This is the practice phase of the process. Here, the teacher's message and purpose is: "I will observe

while you show me. Demonstrate to me that you understand." Or, "I will give you practice as an individual student, with a partner or with a small group." Or, "We will do this together until you get it." Take note of the adverse during the direct instruction phase where the teacher's communication is: "I'll do or I'll show you while you observe and look on."

Teachers utilize the guided practice time to identify and observe if any student is in need of assistance or support. Teachers must be alert and attentive to students' body language, the non-verbal signals to help pick up on unspoken clues of their students' lack of understanding or challenges. Effective teachers are perceptive and geared to listen carefully to students, to their verbal responses, their questions and their answers. This level of listening is necessary to correct a problem, or eliminate any misinformation or confusion, and to also affirm and reinforce that the student is headed in the right direction towards positive progression. Throughout this observant and watchful process, immediate feedback is the teacher's gift to students leading them to improvement and becoming more productive.

Every student needs feedback. Feedback is the "breakfast of champions" and is critically important in improving student performance. When teachers underscore what is right and wrong, or good and bad about their students' instructional work, this assessment helps students to see how they can improve and make continued progress. Feedback informs students if they are on the right track. It builds confidence, sparks motivation to learn and helps students become more reflective and thoughtful. Because of feedback, students have the opportunity to think about what they can do correctively, differently or what they need to do to strengthen their performance.

Caring, competent and conscientious teachers are keenly attentive in identifying students who are having difficulty, whether the students are black, white, Hispanic, Asian, students with special disabilities, or English Language Learners. These teachers' compassion compels them to intervene and to fiercely provide the needed feedback, support, extra time and extra instruction their students need.

Independent Practice
Independent practice is the part of the planned learning experience where students are expected to work with little to no assistance from the teacher. It is the time when students work toward mastery of the desired learning objective presented in the lesson, showing the teacher what they have learned and achieved. Here the teacher's message is: "Show me what you know." Essentially, "Show me that you got it!" The teacher's role in independent practice is to support students as a facilitator. Students apply the skills and knowledge learned during the class learning experiences and display their competencies. Teachers are still expected to be vigilant and alert to students' progress during independent practice to provide the necessary support and encouragement to strengthen learning.

If students are going to retain what they are expected to learn, they must have an opportunity to practice and examine the work and be able to process it on their own. Independent practice gives students the space and time for their natural curiosity to probe, test and investigate their conclusions from multiple angles and perspectives. This can be accomplished individually, in pairs, or in small groups.

What is extremely important with respect to the direct instruction, guided practice and independent practice learning experiences, is that they must be thoughtfully planned, intentional in their delivery, and tightly aligned to the state curriculum. These essential activities, when prepared and executed effectively, are a love thing!

Classroom Management
Classroom management is a love thing! It is an instructional and management thing. It sets the table and atmosphere for learning with the overarching spirit of treating students with dignity, respect and value. Teachers play various roles in a typical classroom, but surely, one of the most important is that of classroom manager.

Effective classroom management allows for the class to function where maximum learning can occur. The most pragmatic approach in classroom management is always preventive and proactive. Thinking and planning ahead is far more efficient and sensible than corrective disciplinary measures after the fact.

As I visited successful classrooms over the years, there were four prevalent components present and predominant as teachers created a businesslike, conducive environment for learning: 1) Caring & Positive Relationships, 2) Appropriate Procedures, Routines and Rules, 3) Skillful Disciplinary Interventions, and 4) Effective Delivery of Instruction. With careful, intentional and skillful integration of these key elements in the classroom, teachers' effectiveness would be enhanced; a healthy learning climate would be promoted; and the prospect of student achievement would greatly increase.

Developing **caring and positive relationships** with students is necessary in effective classroom management. The well-being of both students and teachers are crucial in teaching and learning. John Maxwell once said, "People don't care how much you know until they know how much you care." This reality focuses on the quality and power of the teacher-student relationship as the cornerstone for classroom management strategies.

When students enter the classroom, teachers are often unaware of their students' home life or living situations. Therefore, it is necessary for teachers to connect with their students and work diligently to build a relationship where students feel important, valued, and confidence is restored and increased. The degree of student progress and success in the classroom will be immensely influenced by the level of teacher-student relationship. Caring and positive relationships are, indeed, essential in the classroom! Teaching and learning will not be as effective if teachers do not exhibit genuine care and love for their students and know them as individuals. The clarion message for all educators is before you can "Bloom," you have to "Maslow!" In other words, basic human needs must be considered and addressed by the teacher before student learning can occur. Teachers must understand their students' circumstances, who they are as individuals, and what they are facing before they can effectively participate and learn. It is critical to establish and nurture a connection, a collaboration, and a bond.

As teachers pursue and advance their academic goals, they must take time to understand the social and emotional dynamics of each student and provide the needed support, encouragement and guidance required for students to press through and press forward. Students will strive and accelerate only in an environment where they experience warmth and love from caring adults. You can't fake it! Only genuine goodwill, kindness and care can break through the confusion, chaos and crisis that hinder many students' lives. Teachers can and do make a tremendous difference when students feel accepted, appreciated, valued and supported.

Kids need empathy and compassion! It is important for teachers to understand what is going on in their students' lives. Get to know them — not just in the classroom, but outside, in the hallway, in the cafeteria, at athletic events, school dances, talent shows, drill team competitions, the drama club, band, choir, and cheer squad performances. Cleo Davis and Winifred Corbin were such great teachers to me, extending themselves to provide the time and concern to see through my young challenges to ultimately reveal my worth and potential. Your love can do the same for your students!

Appropriate Procedures, Routines and Rules. The number one classroom problem is not discipline, but the lack of procedures and routines, emphatically proclaimed by Harry Wong. He states that most classroom behavior problems are caused and elevated when the teacher fails to thoroughly explain, teach, model, rehearse and reinforce how students are expected to follow their classroom procedures and rules. Research has repeatedly shown that highly effective teachers must be intentional and resolute in spending much of their first couple of weeks in the school year teaching and practicing classroom procedures and rules. They understand that they have to be steadfast and single-minded in putting in the work upfront, laying the foundation in order to establish the desired classroom standards and expectations.

Effective teachers manage their classrooms with procedures, rules and routines. They focus heavily on establishing and reinforcing practices so the class can operate in a respectable and orderly manner. These skillful teachers focus intently on ensuring students understand the expected behaviors and will practice and rehearse these everyday norms until students "get it right" and it becomes a habit and routine in the classroom. It is vital that students know what is expected of them. So it is essential to teach them what to do, when to do it, how to do it and where to go while in the classroom. These expectations save as much as one hour of instructional time each week or seventy-two hours of instructional time each school year. When teachers teach and practice and students understand and perform appropriately, there is a climate of safety and the classroom environment is more productive and orderly. "Classroom management is built from the ground up so that most classroom problems do not occur," (Jones). When the procedures and rules are clear, fair, understandable and have a sensible, meaningful purpose at its core, the classroom environment will be more conducive for student learning.

For example, in the development of classroom procedures and rules, teachers must give careful and complete thought as to how they want their students to enter the classroom; to get immediately to work; where to find the warm-up activity in the classroom; what to do when they are late to class; coming to attention; when they want to answer a question; what to do when they don't understand or are having difficulty; exchanging papers; getting into small groups; participating in a class discussion or small group discussion; moving about the classroom; taking turns speaking; turning in homework; responding to a fire drill; when there is a school-wide announcement; when they need to go to the restroom; what to do when they finish an assignment early; when the bell rings; when they are dismissed from class; when they are absent and return to class; in addition to other procedures and rules.

To be clear, the posting and announcing of procedures and rules are not enough to create the needed student responses nor establish the desired classroom environment. They are necessary, but not enough! The teaching of the classroom procedures and rules is the vital part. There must be appropriate and consistent teacher behavior, conduct and practices associated with the posting and announcing of the procedures and rules to make them stick and ultimately, make a difference. Teacher action, performance and habits are profoundly required to enforce and reinforce what is expected to create the needed classroom climate.

Teachers must remember that no distinguishable, substantial teaching or learning will take place when there is constant struggling in disciplining students. There will be significant loss of engaged instructional time and student achievement when classroom disruptions, distractions and interruptions consistently impair the teaching and learning process. Teaching and learning takes place when students see and understand why the procedures, rules and routines benefit their learning and progress. This occurs when teacher behaviors and actions are firmly aligned with the communicated expectations and standards.

Possible Rules
Ideally, Class Rules should be easy to follow, and posted for students to see. One of the important aspects to writing effective Classroom Rules is to keep them simple. They should be broad enough to cover a variety of circumstances and situations in the classroom, but specific enough to eliminate any confusion or ambiguity in desired behavior, like the following:

1. **Follow Teacher Directions**
   Following directions is an important ability to practice in everyday life in order to become productive. Following directions can impact personal, small group or classroom safety, increase the learning of the curriculum standards and the essential knowledge and skills, and can clearly influence academic performances. Students who follow classroom and school directions demonstrate that they are understanding,

obliging, cooperative, intelligent, team players and are also dependable, a trait needed in collaboration and working within teams.

2. **Bring Required Materials to Class Every Day**
Students are expected to come to class daily prepared with all of the required materials (books, pens, paper, laptop, etc.). These resources are needed by the students in order to become successful in the classroom. Students are not expected to disturb or interrupt the teacher, other students, or the class to borrow items they forgot or neglected to bring to class. Students are expected to have all of their materials each day so they may participate fully in the learning opportunities planned by their teacher.

3. **Keep Hands, Feet, and Objects to Self**
It is vital that students respect the personal space of others in the classroom and in the school. It is required and necessary that students keep their hands, feet and objects to themselves at all times to demonstrate respect for their classmates, their teacher, and themselves. This requirement is a life-long social skill that students must accept and achieve in order to form and maintain appropriate relationships.

4. **No Food, Drink, Head Gear, or Electronics**
Eating and drinking should be reserved for lunchtime and not the classroom. However, exceptions should be made for students with medical needs. The wearing of headgear (like hats or hoods) is prohibited because it can be a distraction in class, block another student's view and can obscure parts of a student's face, making it difficult to spot an intruder or a student who has done something inappropriate. We are preparing students for career and college readiness. In addition, when class is in session, cell phones and other electronic devices (MP3 players, Air Pods, tablets, etc.) must be turned off. These devices can be a distraction and a

disruption to the learning environment for the teacher, student and other classmates in the classroom.

5. **Attend to Personal Needs Before Class**
Students are urged to use the restroom or stop at their locker before arriving to class to avoid interruptions or disruptions to the class and to increase instructional time and student engagement.

One of the greatest gifts that a caring, professional educator can give to their students on a daily basis is a positive, encouraging and productive learning environment. One vital element to achieve this is the establishment and reinforcement of procedures, routines and rules in the classroom. Teachers must create a climate where amazing instruction is possible and student achievement can be accelerated for every student.

Skillful Disciplinary Interventions
In his book, *Tools for Teaching,* Dr. Fred Jones indicated that 95% of inappropriate student behavior in the classroom is non-serious, but annoying. How true! As a result, he cites and recommends the diligent use of some very practical, evidence-based intervention strategies to curb improper student behavior while keeping in mind the importance of disciplining with dignity.

1. The Look
One of the most effective non-verbal classroom management techniques is "the look." Yes, the infamous stare! What a handy weapon to have in your classroom management arsenal. I have found, through my teaching experience and the numerous classroom observations as an administrator, how skillful classroom teachers can prompt and quicken a distracted student back into the rhythm of the instructional lesson without saying a single word. It is amazing how effective a firm, no-nonsense facial expression or gaze serves as a signal to the inattentive student that they are off-task, distracted, disruptive, have their head in the clouds or doing something they shouldn't. The "look" projects a serious, insistent warning to the preoccupied or

wayward student. It does not express anger, aggressiveness or hostility to the student, but its purpose is to quickly redirect in a stern, calm and resolute manner. The "look" is not the Gomer Pyle demeanor with Golly! or Shazam! behind it, but a look that conveys that the teacher means "business." In order for the "look" to be effective, it must have a persistent history of consequences behind it in the classroom to achieve the desired impact.

2. The Pause
The pause is a tried and true, dependable approach to integrate in the teacher's repertoire of classroom management techniques. This useful method of strategic silence for a few moments geared towards a student who is distracted, disruptive, daydreaming or disengaged can reconnect and prompt the student to return to instructional engagement. An occasional two or three second decisive, distinct pause can break up the monotone, mundane teacher's voice and the rapid fire of information to keep students attentive, interested, on their toes, and to help them stay on task.

3. Proximity Control – Management By Walking Around (MBWA)
Proximity control or classroom management by walking around is a strategy where teachers decrease the distance between themselves and their students. The power of a teacher's physical location along with their watchfulness and diligence in the classroom can have a significant effect on students' engagement, motivation and achievement. Bottom line, where a teacher stands, moves and teaches in the classroom can make a tremendous difference in curbing inappropriate behavior, breaking up talkative combinations of students and reengaging students. Circulating around the classroom as you teach helps keep students focused and on task in a non-confrontational way.

Each teacher must ensure that the seating arrangements in the classroom will allow for ease of movement. From the front of class to the back and anywhere in between, the teacher must be able to move quickly and covertly to redirect students back on task. Without skipping a beat or losing precious instructional time, the teacher must be able to move closer to students who might be distracted, goofing around or just need some help. Proximity control is not an oppressive law enforcement surveillance with the rigidity of policing, but it is an excellent opportunity for intentional interaction, encouragement, connection, guidance and support to students. While moving around the classroom, the teacher can monitor student work, their progress, ask questions, provide needed feedback, and give encouragement. The teacher can also request students to explain their answers, justify their responses, give examples, illustrations or ask the student to summarize what he/she just learned. A teacher's physical presence is both crucial and powerful. It sends a compelling message of care – caring enough to be attentive and diligent while encouraging and supporting students to higher achievement.

4. Preventive Seating
Preventive seating is another effective action a teacher can employ to minimize and reduce disruptions before they even occur in class. It is implemented in the classroom for the purpose of decreasing student disruptions, developing appropriate student conduct, and accelerating increased student success. A teacher can greatly reduce inappropriate conduct in class by knowing their students well enough. This requires the teacher to be proactive and attentive enough to make the decision to redirect a student to another seat. Preventive seating is conducted by relocating an identified student to a seat where the probability of interruptions will be lessened.

5. Call Students By Name
Calling students by their name is so obvious, fundamental and basic to classroom interventions and the promotion of a healthy classroom culture. Additionally, pronouncing students' names correctly is equally important. Failure to do so or repeatedly mispronouncing a student's name can have a lasting, negative impact. Teachers will find some students' names difficult to pronounce, especially on the first day of school, but repeated mispronunciation can be considered disrespectful, contentious and racially unfriendly. The significance of communicating students' names properly conveys respect and value, and also helps students

feel important as individuals in the classroom. Not only does calling a student by their name connect the teacher with their students, it also increases trust, communication, and accountability with the likelihood of students responding positively to the teacher's requests. Teachers are most effective when they know their students and call them by their name. When teachers convey value and trust toward their students, they become easier to teach.

6. Use Humor
Humor, when incorporated and delivered in a spirit of love and instruction, can be an effective classroom management tool in the teacher's toolbox. Humor is a legitimate icebreaker, stress reducer, and a vehicle to increase optimism and confidence. Adding appropriate humor in the classroom can build connection and advance learning because it is fun and engaging. Humor can quickly lighten a tense or difficult situation in the classroom and can shift the atmosphere in a positive direction. Before using humor, it is extremely important for teachers to strongly consider whether it will embarrass, insult or upset a student. Humor should never be hostile, offensive, demeaning or hurtful to students, but something that everyone can laugh at, enjoy and benefit from. Humor should never be used as a revenge tactic or power move by the teacher but rather as an opportunity to help students gain a better perspective and outlook, replacing frustration and anger with laughter and cooperation.

In summary, the research over the past 30 years indicates that the teacher's: 1) Knowledge of Content, 2) Effective Instructional Planning, 3) Skillful Use of Different Instructional Resources, 4) Skillful Use of Instructional Strategies, 5) Effective Classroom Management Techniques, and 6) Humanistic Skills are critical ingredients of effective teaching. It is extremely important that teachers are keenly aware of these prevailing evidence-based instructional practices and incorporate these effective strategies in the classroom. Student achievement is optimized when love is at the core of teachers' hard work and heart work and effective integration of the aforementioned instructional components. Effective instruction is indeed a love thing and teachers must be committed to incorporating these vital action steps in the classroom in order to increase student learning. They must have an unwavering belief that every student has the ability and thus will learn at high levels. It's a love thing!

"Without data, you're just another person with an opinion."
— Edwards Deming

Chapter 8
The Use of Data in Decision Making

Data! Data! Data! Talking about a love thing — identifying the needed data and using it in the school's decision making process is a love thing! If you truly care for your students, staff, and school community, you must use data to guide decisions and actions that drive positive change and raise achievement.

Using data and intensely applying its findings, in my view, is always about caring deeply enough to improve and transform the school to a more positive and productive place of safety, synergy and success. You cannot move or advance your school as an organization of change and exceptional achievement until you identify and focus on the essential pieces of informational data to help you make smarter and more informed decisions. With that acknowledgment, leaders must give data a "vital, vibrant, valuable voice" in the schoolhouse to make a difference and to establish a data-driven culture. "Data in a school is the new oil," expressed by Clive Humby. It is extremely valuable, rich and needed to fuel the decisions and direction for improvement. In essence, "data really powers everything that we do," as Jeff Weiner conveys.

The importance of having and using data cannot be overstated. Your school's journey towards improvement begins by gathering, examining, reporting and decisively acting upon the right data to make crucial decisions. That is the goal! That is the mission! The use of school data is not a petty, minor, shallow exercise nor a hit or miss effort. It is a thoughtful, comprehensive, deliberate and on-going approach. "Data by itself is useless and it is only useful when we apply it," (Park). Your school will not move forward until you address data decisively, boldly, consistently and collaboratively by allowing the data to inform and inspire your next steps and actions.

But you must possess the courage and bold leadership to act on the information.

The biggest challenge and hurdle to becoming a data-driven school culture is the failure of leadership to put data consistently in front of the school family (teachers, students, parents and other stakeholders) and to make it central to the school's progress. Evaluating student and school progress is a crucial part of instruction. Without key informational data, school leaders and teachers would be walking and whistling in the dark, operating in a thick fog and lacking the directional focus needed to drive instructional decisions to foster accountability. As Edwards Deming stated, "Without data, you're just another person with an opinion" and having an opinion or possessing strong feelings are never enough to lead to breakthrough student results. "There are lies, damned lies and statistics," Mark Twain once said. So let's be led by the statistics, the facts.

School leaders must subscribe and adhere to the behavior of "Keeping Score." That is constantly reviewing, studying and discussing with stakeholders and partners the school data, and focusing energies and responsibilities to finding solutions and opportunities to improve the school's overall achievement.

Throughout my career, I have found the importance of routinely asking key probing questions to guide decisions and actions while assessing the needs, challenges and successes of students, groups of students, grade levels, teachers and subject areas. It is essential to become cognizant of where students are improving and where students are not progressing and why. Asking the right questions and digging deeper into the data can offer insight and perspectives to the factors behind student improvement or lack of growth, arming you with the opportunity to find solutions.

It's important to ask data questions such as, *"Where are we now?"* As Jim Collins stated in his book, *Good to Great*, "confronting the realities of the school is crucial." Educators must be willing to acknowledge and act upon the *"Now!"* element. You absolutely cannot make a series of good decisions without confronting the brutal facts of your school. This is a must in order to set priorities, goals and action steps for the future and to find solutions. When school leaders examine the truth of the school with honesty and transparency, better decisions will evolve. It is unreasonable to think that leaders can make good decisions in the blind or without a genuine analysis of the data. Data will help school leaders see things more clearly, which is sometimes a painful perspective of the school's current reality. Charles Dickens once said, "Take nothing on its looks: Take everything on evidence." There is no better rule!

Where do we want to go from here? How will we better serve and support the constituents in the school? How will we better deliver excellence to all of our students regardless of their demographics or zip code? How do we define excellence? How will we ensure equity, fairness and quality access in our school community? What do we individually and collectively need to do to improve achievement for all students? How will we get there as a team and as a school? How do we support and assist new teachers, struggling teachers and co-teachers?

What do we want to achieve? What are the learning targets? What measurable goals do we want to accomplish? Are instructional lessons aligned with the state standards? How do we know? How will we monitor and gauge learning? How often will we assess student progress? What tools will we use to measure progress? What are our next steps? What essential action steps must we take as a result of the data? Which instructional strategies seem to work best? Who is responsible for certain action steps? How will we know we are there? How will we respond in our school when students are having difficulty? What will we do to ensure their success? What intervention, support and extra time will we provide to meet and exceed the standards? How can we keep the positive momentum going?

These are just a few questions to guide better instructional responses in a comprehensive way.

As the school's instructional leader, you must possess diagnostic and investigative skills similar to a primary care physician (PCP), a doctor, or a general practitioner. A PCP starts with a thorough review of the patient's medical history, interviewing and asking relevant questions of the patient while examining and diagnosing the current condition, illnesses, and injuries. When the PCP believes sufficient information has been gathered, then a prescription for treatment and needed care is determined to improve the patient's health and well-being.

Very similarly, as an instructional leader, you should become *The Primary Care Principal,* responsible for the comprehensive care and well-being of your patients (students, staff and other stakeholders). Like the general practitioner, *The Primary Care Principal* must decide where to intelligently begin by asking the right questions, by looking at the school's history, various school charts, graphs, tables, surveys, and assessments results to pinpoint various needs, then collaborate and coordinate the range of services within the school to meet those varied needs.

As *The Primary Care Principal,* your diagnostic and prescriptive actions are equally comparable and vital. You must examine, analyze and ask probing questions of students, staff, parents, community leaders and other stakeholders through an inquisitive and caring lens to determine the corrective, restorative remedies and practices to improve the school's overall health. School leaders must explore the information from all angles, be armed with the appropriate facts, consult with other relevant professionals such as teachers, instructional specialists, other administrators, central office leaders and educational consultants (to name a few) and make evidence-based decisions from the best information, knowledge and practices available.

Like a physician, school leaders must never be hasty in making decisions because the life and fitness of the school are too critical to be impulsive and rash. The stakes are too high! The well-being and health of the school are far too vital to be impetuous and abrupt. School leaders must be thoughtful and detail-oriented in deciding the best course of action.

School data must become your *BFF*, **B**est **F**riend to move **F**orward. Key data to improve the instructional and operational practices, especially in the areas of school leadership, climate and culture, instructional focus, extra help opportunities, teamwork and increased student achievement, are crucial.

School data is far more than test scores. It involves and measures the entire school enterprise, its aspirations, its systems, processes and structures. Leaders may find in their conscientious and thoughtful deep data dive that the school's prevailing practices, policies and patterns are provoking the problems and pain in the school. It could be us! Our conduct, the behavior of the adults in the school, could be the obstacle to becoming more productive. School leaders may also find that the school's trends, tendencies and tactics may trigger the troubles, traumas and turbulence prohibiting the school from reaching its full potential of excellence.

Your aim as a school leader is to serve all students well by creating a school environment promoting and ensuring equity and excellence for all. A deep detail-oriented data dive must be your "BFF" and championed on your agenda. If the data reveals that staff conduct is contrary to equity, excellence and the school's mission, then courage and conviction are needed to find new ways and patterns of direction, guidance and support to create the positive change necessary to achieve breakthrough student success.

The creation of a data team is a key element in communicating school ownership, collaboration and transparency in changing the climate of the school. It may consist of administrators, department chairs and other teacher leaders. The message that radiates with the establishment of a data team is that no longer will data be handled by a few individuals in isolation but now by a more comprehensive, inclusive and expanded team of school leaders. Data is now at the forefront and central to everyone in the school. Data helps the entire school community become more keenly aware of the valuable information needed for improvement. Additionally, data and the data team create a climate of accountability ensuring that everybody, every day is answerable to the results.

Below are some possible areas of school data to examine in your audit overview in pursuit of equity and excellence. Frequent data examination of these targets and others will expose your focus and commitment to creating a more positive and productive change in serving your school. So collect data that is targeted, useful and specific to making key decisions.

• **Grade Level Student Population** A. Demographics 1. Male 2. Female 3. Black 4. White 5. Hispanic 6. Asian 7. English Language Learner 8. Students with Disabilities 9. Socio Economic Condition	• **Dropout Rates** A. Demographics 1. Male 2. Female 3. Black 4. White 5. Hispanic 6. Asian 7. English Language Learner 8. Students with Disabilities 9. Socio Economic Condition
• **Student Attendance** A. Demographics 1. Male 2. Female 3. Black 4. White 5. Hispanic 6. Asian 7. English Language Learner 8. Students with Disabilities 9. Socio Economic Condition	• **School Suspensions** ISS/OSS/Long-Term Suspension/Expulsion A. Demographics 1. Male 2. Female 3. Black 4. White 5. Asian 6. Hispanic 7. English Language Learner 8. Students with Disabilities 9. Socio Economic Condition

The Use of Data in Decision Making

• **Teacher Attendance** A. Demographics 1. Male 2. Female 3. Black 4. White 5. Hispanic 6. Asian 7. Probationary 8. Continuing Contract	• **End-of-Course State Standards Results** A. Demographics 1. Male 2. Female 3. Black 4. White 5. Hispanic 6. Asian 7. English Language Learner 8. Students with Disabilities 9. Socio Economic Condition
• **Teacher Licensure** Teacher Quality Review A. Probationary B. Continuing Contract	• **District Benchmark Results** A. Cluster Common Assessments B. Classroom Formative Assessments • Demographics 1. Male 2. Female 3. Black 4. White 5. Hispanic 6. Asian 7. English Language Learner 8. Students with Disabilities 9. Socio Economic Condition

• **Graduation Rates** Standard Diploma/Advanced Diploma/GED A. Demographics 1. Male 2. Female 3. Black 4. White 5. Hispanic 6. Asian 7. English Language Learner 8. Students with Disabilities 9. Socio Economic Condition	• **Student Grades** • By Teacher Content Cluster PLC A. Interim Grades B. Quarterly Grades C. Semester Grades D. Final Grades E. Demographics 1. Male 2. Female 3. Black 4. White 5. Hispanic 6. Asian 7. English Language Learner 8. Students with Disabilities 9. Socio Economic Condition
• **Rigorous Courses** Talented & Gifted/AP/IB/Dual Enrollment/ Honors Classes/Foreign Languages A. Demographics 1. Male 2. Female 3. Black 4. White 5. Hispanic 6. Asian 7. English Language Learner 8. Students with Disabilities 9. Socio Economic Condition	• **Special Education Data** A. Demographics 1. Male 2. Female 3. Black 4. White 5. Hispanic 6. Asian 7. English Language Learner 8. Socio Economic Condition

• **School Discipline** ISS/OSS/Long-Term Suspensions/Expulsions A. Demographics 1. Male 2. Female 3. Black 4. White 5. Hispanic 6. Asian 7. English Language Learner 8. Students with Disabilities 9. Socio Economic Condition	• **Career and Technical Education Enrollment** Receipt of Certification A. Demographics 1. Male 2. Female 3. Black 4. White 5. Hispanic 6. Asian 7. English Language Learner 8. Students with Disabilities 9. Socio Economic Condition
• **Representation in Student Organizations** Student Government, National Honors Society, Beta Club, Cheerleaders, Debate Club, Athletic Teams, JROTC, etc. A. Demographics 1. Male 2. Female 3. Black 4. White 5. Hispanic 6. Asian 7. English Language Learner 8. Students with Disabilities 9. Socio Economic Condition	

As the Executive Director of Secondary and Career and Technical Education of Mooresville Graded School District, the data categories above were instrumental in uncovering the gaps and shortcomings of our district. Even though Mooresville was considered a moderately performing district (ranked 38 out of 115 school districts) in North Carolina's End of Course Results in 2008, the performances of our demographics were significantly lagging. In the words of our superintendent, Dr. Mark Edwards, "average is never our goal." Our new energy and effort as a district was to become the number one performing district in North Carolina and to achieve excellence and equity in our student performances.

We did not and could not accomplish this noble aim with our white children alone or our affluent students alone. We had to expect and insist that we widen our lens and deepen our reach as a school community. "Every Child, Every Day" was the district's motto, but in reality, in too many instances in our schools and classrooms were we operating more like, "some of the children, some of the time." We exhibited "stinking thinking" (deficit thinking) with a significant portion of students and we needed to closely examine our beliefs, decisions and practices. We had to take a hard look at some of our attitudes, practices and biases which were hindering some students' progress. Many of our minority, SWDs, and impoverished students were not succeeding at appropriate standards. The brutal facts of the data were a jolt to some of us and a wake-up call to better serve all of our students! This revealing data placed a brilliant floodlight on our deficiencies and became the ignition to change how we did business going forward. Our superintendent, central office leadership and building leadership had to exhibit increased leadership in love, care, higher expectations, accountability and courage to change the district's performance.

Leadership matters! Courage, consistency and commitment matter! It is always the behaviors and actions of school leaders that determine whether or not opportunity gaps are closed and all children learn at high levels. What school leaders do as a result of data matters greatly. The reason why some schools succeed in closing or eliminating opportunity gaps has less to do with skill. It has more to do with the ***will*** and the conviction of leadership. School leaders must have a strong willingness to commit to the success of all of the students in their school. They do whatever it takes to support students' success with boldness, accountability and with a moral imperative to meet the instructional needs of all of their students to close glaring disparities.

As James Joseph Scheurich and Linda Skala stated in their book, *Leadership for Equity and Excellence*, "The success of our society will soon be directly dependent on our ability as school leaders and educators to be successful with children of color and children from low socio-economic backgrounds." If school leaders are sincere and committed to the process of using data frequently and routinely to uncover flaws and failures in the work and demonstrate the courage and conviction to devise and enact new strategies to accelerate student achievement, then we are on our way to excellence and equity. Amen!

I recall an illustration I read several years ago. I have altered it a bit to sharpen the message.

Imagine driving your SUV, **School Utility Vehicle,** with your **school** on a long, 180-day journey from September to June. During this exciting, arduous trip, you and the school encounter and experience many twists and turns, bumps and bruises, ups and downs, potholes, flashing lights, traffic jams, poor visibility, fog, Stop signs, Yield signs, road blocks, one-way streets, seat belt reminders, and more.

Now envision your inability as a school leader to view the SUV dashboard panel with its many essential gauges. The dashboard panel has instruments and dials that provide clear and crucial information, like updates and warnings that you need to be aware of to navigate your way. Without the dashboard's valuable information, how can you plan for a successful trip?

How can you ensure safe travel without the dashboard's indicators to monitor progress and to show you the way? How can you accurately navigate toward the desired destination? Stay on course and make adjustments where necessary? How would you know that an instrument is getting ready to malfunction (oil gauge, gas gauge, tire gauge, etc.)? Where can you stop for fuel or for help?

Additionally, it would also be extremely difficult to proceed in your SUV with your school without the **GPS:** your vision, mission statement and school goals to chart the course; the **speedometer** to provide on-going literacy and numeracy data results; the **fuel gauge** to assess student and teacher attendance; the **oil pressure gauge** to measure student discipline data; the **temperature gauge** to keep you apprised of the graduation rate and dropout rate; the **tachometer** to monitor the GAP Group Results, the school's demographics data points; the **voltmeter gauge** to assess the participation and progress of the AP & Talent and Gifted Program; and the **odometer** to measure the strategic use of technology in the classroom.

How can you determine progress without the dashboard? How would you know which students are struggling? Which students are not? Which curriculum standards are students having difficulty with? How can we know that we are on track and heading in the right direction? How are we performing in the area of equity and excellence? How quickly can we provide targeted intervention and support?

Leading a school without the needed dashboard data and measurements is highly risky, reckless and full of uncertainty in this long school travel. Keeping score and a watchful eye on the measurement of student progress and achievements are critically important.

I am reminded of the time I was returning from visiting my (then) fiancé in Roanoke, Virginia in my 1973 Chevy Laguna

The Use of Data in Decision Making

Sedan. What a classic! But it was a huge gas guzzler! Well, prior to this trip, my gas gauge became inoperative. Instead of getting it serviced and repaired, I hurried to Roanoke and upon my return from the "Star City," you guessed it — the inevitable happened. I ran out of gas about fifteen miles from my home in Richmond. I was stranded in the dark on Highway 64 East and had to walk three miles to the nearest gas station. I knew I was taking a chance, but I was hoping and gambling nonetheless. My good sense left me and I depended on luck and hope. As you know, "hope is not a plan."

The point of this story is there are school leaders who also operate on hope and luck with partial information and no good sense. They function in the blind without the key data needed to make sound decisions toward student success. Without big data, one would feel like being in the middle of a freeway, blind and deaf, describes Geoffrey Moore, an American business consultant.

I am sure you have heard the statement by Peter Drucker, "What gets measured gets done." It's a very profound explanation proclaiming that frequent analysis and interaction with data will keep school leaders focused on the "main things," the essential facts needed to make better decisions. The best decision-makers in our schools are always armed with the best information and data! Data helps school leaders and the data team to see things more clearly, sometimes a painful perspective of the school's current reality. Identifying and using data in the school's decision making process is a love thing. It takes love, care, courage and commitment to your school's performances to lift your school to higher levels of service and achievement.

What we have learned is that school leadership must give data an enormous voice and a critical place in the school in order to make smarter decisions and to ignite a deeper impact in the school's outcomes. The thoughtful, consistent and strategic use of data along with the intense, courageous application of the findings is a love thing which can transform a school to exceptional improvement. So keep data at the heart of your decisions and work. Use data to champion the way forward in your school! Because the love of your students and their progress will demand leaders to embrace school data and to use its findings to make informed instructional decisions to improve student achievements.

"You will either step forward into growth or you will step backwards into safety."
— Abraham Maslow

Chapter 9
Care Enough to Confront

My focus in this segment is highlighting the value and importance of exhibiting "leadership courage." On behalf of your students and staff, school leaders must demonstrate resolute and boldness in times of challenge and turbulence. In these times, effective leaders set themselves apart by having the ability to become comfortable, intentional and focused when conducting courageous, and sometimes uncomfortable, conversations. Courage, inner strength, and determination have always been associated with leadership.

The administrator's ability to successfully address staff performance issues is crucial to school culture and achievement. Too often the path of safety, least resistance and popularity are chosen by school leaders, instead of addressing the challenges that negatively impact the school's performance and effectiveness. I have worked with principals and assistant principals who were very nice people — caring, hardworking, and knowledgeable, but lacked the heart, the will and the grit to make the necessary decisions to facilitate positive change in their respective schools.

In the school environment, leaders will have to work through various irritations, agitations and aggravations within the building to establish and maintain a collective understanding and commitment to the school's vision and goals of the school by all staff members. Leaders must address any staff conduct that has abandoned or dropped the organization's mission and standards. Schools need bold change agents to improve the learning environment and culture. Some leaders I have observed over the years displayed obvious signs of an internal civil war raging within them. In turn, this conflict paused, and in some instances, hindered, conversations that needed to emerge. These leaders struggled with protecting people's feelings — not wanting anyone to feel bad or become angry as a result of some hard truths. They were sometimes conflicted about whether to be popular or be effective in the school.

I learned early in my administrative career that you "get what you tolerate." If you want people to win, then care enough to confront or in the words of John Maxwell, "clarify." If you desire positive change in your school, then recognize the importance and need to conduct courageous conversations and take bold, affirmative steps.

I found that when the leader steps up with both love and courage, the staff will:

- Clearly understand the school's expectations and standards and behave in a manner that is in alignment with school requirements and norms.
- Create a school environment where improper staff behavior will be reduced, minimized, or eliminated and a greater commitment to the school's mission, work and responsibilities will occur.
- Exhibit increased confidence and respect for the school's administration and colleagues.

Caring enough to clarify is absolutely necessary in transforming a school and building school synergy. As the school leader, you must have the heart and tenacity required to hold the line on behaviors that are contrary to the school's mission and values. You are the school's "Standard Bearer," the champion and primary mover and shaker in the building. You carry the school's banner more proudly and profoundly than anyone else! You set the direction as to what is acceptable and what is not. Moreover, you determine how the school will conduct business and operate as a learning community.

If work expectations and norms are established and communicated to staff, then it is up to you as the leader of the school to verify that the work and standards are being met at the required level. In the subtle words of Ronald Reagan, "trust but verify." Get to the root cause of the matter. Dig deep, then act. If you fail to appropriately confront staff for not complying with the systems, processes and structures that have been erected for school improvement, then you will achieve the outcome that results from the standards not being followed. You will get what you allow!

As important as this leadership trait is to the success of schools, why do some school leaders ignore and evade confronting improper staff conduct? Especially when the behavior opposes what is good for the school and good for the children? What paralyzes administrators is quite obvious. It is fear! Fear is the underlying factor. Fear is the elephant in the room. Fear is the key obstacle and barrier preventing these conversations from occurring. It is fear that causes the school leader to look the other way. Some administrators fear reprisal or blow back from specific teachers or groups of teachers. They fear being disliked, disapproved, criticized, rebuked, vilified or rejected.

"What you tolerate will continue," said Sheila Wray Gregoire. When administrators continually fail to take affirmative actions to ensure adherence and alignment to school standards, problems worsen and are likely to be repeated. The school climate will suffer, student performance will decrease, and the school's leadership credibility and reliability will be diminished.

The lack of courage and leadership, which allows adverse and conflicting behaviors to remain, will eventually take hold and lessen school progress. Leadership is expected to shoulder the responsibility for what happens in the school. Leadership sets the tone and determines how business is conducted by words and actions. The way forward and through always rests with the school leadership as they move to achieve the school's vision, mission and goals.

Have you heard of the musical artist, James Fortune? He had a radio program and during a segment of it, he'd present various scenarios and ask, "If this happens to you, what cha'gonna do?" Listeners had the opportunity to call in to give their responses. Here are some possible school situations for you to think about how you would respond:

What cha'gonna do if...

- You do not have "all hands (teachers) on deck" between classes (hall duty)?
- A teacher is absent and there are no emergency plans?
- Poor student performances are posted on the math benchmark assessment?
- School data reveals that very few African-American and Hispanic students are enrolled in your Talented and Gifted Classes and AP courses?
- A staff member is repeatedly late for work and/or meetings?
- A teacher has excessive student disciplinary referrals?
- Weekly student grades are not posted into the parent portal as required?
- Lesson plans are not submitted to the administrator/department chair for review by the designated date?
- The word wall, student data wall, or student work are not displayed in the classroom?

What cha'gonna do?

The following is a conversation format I found and used as a guide in leading discussions with staff members. It has been very useful and helpful in framing my discussions with staff.

The example below addresses the issue of tardiness in the workplace, but one can insert any scenario listed above or others to practice using the format.

I Need Your Help!

When You....

Describe the inappropriate behavior. Do your research before conducting the meeting. Have your facts together: include date(s), time(s), etc.

Convey Expectations

Cite School Policy, District Policy, Performance Standards or Job Description

Help Me to Understand

Listen, Listen, Listen

In the Future, You are Expected to …

Give the Person a Game Plan to Fix the Problem

Any Repeat of this Conduct Will Result in…

Or

Failure to Respond Appropriately Will Result in …

Provide Words of Affirmation

I Need Your Help! I Am Counting On You!

Example: Teacher Late to the Workplace

I Need Your Help!	I Need Your Help!
When You…. *Describe the inappropriate behavior. Do your research before conducting the meeting. Have your facts together: include date(s), time(s), etc.*	I observed you when you arrived at school this morning at 8:45 am, well beyond the expected arrival time. As a result, you were unavailable to provide appropriate supervision on the walkway and to receive your first period students. This is unacceptable! This is also a school-wide testing day where the collection, distribution of materials and directing and

	assisting students to their proper testing location were extremely important.
Convey Expectations *Cite School Policy, District Policy, Performance Standards or Job Description*	As stated in our faculty handbook, staff members are expected to arrive at school by 8:15 am and be available at their classroom door by 8:25 am. The administrative team expects "all hands on deck" from staff members during student arrivals and transitions ensuring proper student conduct and safety.
Help Me to Understand *Listen, Listen, Listen*	Help me to understand your late arrival to the school this morning. Are there circumstances I need to be made aware of?
In the Future, You are Expected to … *Give the Person a Game Plan to Fix the Problem*	In the future, you are expected to arrive at the workplace by 8:15 am and be available at your classroom door by 8:25 to provide adequate supervision.

Any Repeat of this Conduct Will Result in…	Any repeat of this conduct will result in further disciplinary action.
Or	Or
Failure to Respond Appropriately Will Result in …	Failure to respond appropriately will not serve in your professional best interest.
Provide Words of Affirmation	You are one of our key mathematics teachers. Your leadership in organizing our intervention plan with Ms. Noel is recognized and appreciated.
I Need Your Help! I Am Counting On You!	I need your help! I stand ready to assist you in any way I can! I am counting on you.

As the school leader, you are quality control and the guardian of the process. In real estate, the three key words are Location! Location! Location! In schools, the key words are Adherence! Adherence! Adherence!

If you know something must change, then also know that it is *you* who must change it. If you ignore, avoid, sidestep or dodge a situation that is not in alignment with your school's mission and values, you just sent out a loud, clear message that it is acceptable to be in direct conflict with the school's mission and values. As a school leader, you must possess the ability to recognize when to stand up. Your job is always to put kids first and to make it crystal clear that there is only one agenda for every classroom in your school and that plan must be driven by the single belief that we serve all of our students really well, regardless of their differences.

In my first year as principal of Henrico High School, our administrative team non-renewed eight teachers. These were good people; however, they did not meet the professional or instructional standards required to continue wearing the "Green and Gold." They did not pass the "litmus test." Would I want my child in their classroom? Believe me, it would have been much easier to close my eyes, look the other way, or use the rationale, "I don't want to hurt their feelings or make them upset," when in fact, it was really my feelings that I wanted to protect. I did not want to get stressed out! These were tough conversations and actions. I discovered that when you prune the relationships around you in your school, you're not just cutting things out; you're making room for growth! You have to make the decision between facilitating growth or enduring grief! After months of intervention, support, guidance and direction, we decided to move forward with dismissal. We lovingly nurtured them to new opportunities!

This reminds me of a story I read of a superintendent of a large school district. One day he met with one of his principals to ask why the children in his school were consistently underperforming. The principal walked the superintendent to the window in his office, pointed to the children entering the school, and said, "You see those poor kids? Most of them have one parent, if that. They can't read. Many are in special ed. Many don't even speak the language. They just aren't going to make it!" This superintendent, after hearing an earful of excuses, fired the principal that day. True story! Wow! What a decision! What a message! This superintendent took action and demonstrated that this principal's "stinking thinking" was unacceptable to elevate the school to growth. If that principal remained, the school was headed to more grief, heartbreak and misery. Growth or Grief! Success or Sadness!

Yet, each one of us has to answer the same question. Every school in America has to answer the same question. Rick DuFour asks, "What will we do when students struggle and have difficulty learning?" This is the million dollar question. Throughout the United States, there are schools that are failing to serve our students really well. And I would say with confidence that these schools did not answer that question very well. The reality is, if we are not winning or achieving with our students, we desperately need to re-examine and rethink our beliefs, our behavior, and our practices.

Leadership is a love thing. Making tough decisions on behalf of students requires courage and love.

"The will to win is important, but the will to prepare is vital."
— Joe Paterno

Chapter 10
Champions are Made in the Off-Season

Athletes use the off-season as a crucial time for targeted growth and preparation. This is the period after the conclusion of a playing season when athletes have a chance to rest, recover, reflect and build a stronger foundation for the next season. Athletes spend much of their time and energy in the off-season strength training, conditioning, and skill developing in order to place themselves and their team in a stronger position for victory for the upcoming season. These conscientious athletes, after analyzing their previous year's performance numbers, identify specific areas of growth and then create an individual plan to successfully enhance their performance and maximize their potential.

The summer off-season for administrators is very similar to athletes. It starts with making a firm, unwavering commitment to becoming a better school leader. This is the first obligation. It then takes form by devoting time, energy and resources to professional growth. This respite after the academic school year starts with honest self-reflection, self-examination, listening to trusted colleagues and mentors, and then deciding on a leadership performance plan for self-improvement. This self-improvement plan should be designed to equip you with increased leadership knowledge and skills which will guide you as you lead your school to exceptional achievement.

I believe that there is one thing that will improve a school when preparing for the upcoming academic school year and that is a better *you*, a better school leader. Investing in your professional growth is crucial for the school leader and the school as a whole. It is vital to continue improving professionally, staying current and relevant, because the educational environment continues to be influenced by new research, new policies, new technologies, erratic politics and unpredictable community issues. Self-improvement is needed in a leader in order to create the positive change and transformation required to boost student success. When leaders commit to learning and growing, they will have a compelling impact on teaching and learning that will elevate the trajectory of a school's performance. Conversely, when the instructional leader stops growing and is reluctant to continue learning, the school becomes stagnant and unproductive. Where there is a lack of growth or professional development, there is no leadership! There is no progress.

While the summer brings a well-deserved break for administrators, it also presents an extraordinary opportunity for growth. When school instructional leaders focus on self-reflection, self-improvement, and make an on-going commitment to their professional growth and the development of their leadership team, they position their school for accelerated growth. Whether participating in summer conferences, workshops, retreats, webinars or reading recommended instructional or leadership books, articles or collaborating with colleagues and mentors, growing and improving professionally are essential to school accomplishment.

As a former high school principal and central office administrator, summer off-seasons were filled with attending and participating in select national and state conferences and inviting key school leaders to join in this collaborative growth experience. This was vital to our continued success as a school and school district. I asked school leaders to lead with me and take more responsibility and ownership in the direction and work of the school. Engaging these pivotal school leaders in an authentic, genuine and collaborative manner was extremely important and essential for collective school improvement. This involvement lifted their leadership, their responsibility and boosted their motivation. They were engaged, empowered, and recognized for their leadership importance and valuable contributions. This collaboration in building leadership capacity gave us a tremendous edge and afforded us the best opportunity to turn vision into reality.

Notable national conferences that greatly contributed to my professional leadership and to our school leaders were the *High Schools That Work National Conference*, the *International Baccalaureate Conference*, and the *National Association of Secondary School Principals*. These experiences were inspiring, engaging and provided the rich golden nuggets needed to enhance our leadership knowledge and skills.

Instructional leaders need a wide range of instructional knowledge and leadership best practices to lead more effectively in changing the educational landscape of a school. As you examine your professional needs and the needs of your school, what leadership knowledge, skills and key instructional practices could be identified to create an individual leadership improvement plan and the plan for your leadership team? Could it be any of these listed below?

1) Technology Integration and Digital Literacy
2) Incorporating High Expectations for All Students
3) Data-Driven Decision Making and Assessment Literacy
4) Creating a More Positive, Responsive and Supportive School Culture
5) Sharpening Our Practices: Improving Professional Learning in School
6) Improving Student Attendance
7) Alternatives to the Traditional College Pathway

8) Nurturing Continuous Growth: Building Leadership Capacity Among Your Staff
9) Improving Teamwork: Strength in Unity
10) Assessing, Monitoring and Supporting Teaching and Learning
11) Developing Effective Communication and Support Within the School Community
12) Improving Students' High Order Thinking Skills
13) Improving Reading Comprehension/The Science of Reading
14) Online and Hybrid Learning in Classroom Instruction
15) Teacher Retention and Shortages

Only through self-reflection and self-assessment can a school leader develop an improvement plan inclusive of the training and targeted learning experiences needed to increase school success. Instructional leadership is hard work and full of challenges and opportunities. The best administrators grow their schools by growing their team. So it is, indeed, essential that the school leader looks for ways to grow and to grow the team. They should be intense and intentional in their commitment to professional development during the academic school year, but especially during the off-season summer months. No matter how good the school performance was the previous year, school leaders are obligated to improve and strive for higher achievement year after year.

As school leaders approach the summer months, I encourage them and their team to use the "off-season" to strengthen professional practices and return to school with increased knowledge, understanding, and confidence in the needed pedagogy to better serve the school community for the upcoming school year. The off-season isn't idle time. It is about intentional preparation, planning, and professional development.

I urge school leaders to be the best they can be by allowing the love for their students and staff to motivate and drive critical investments in professional improvement and growth opportunities. School leaders must be deliberate and intentional in planning learning opportunities. When the school leadership grows, the school grows. If school leaders are not growing and improving, the school will not progress in the manner that will promote increased performance. The moment school leaders stop learning and growing professionally is the time the school community will lack passion, focus and the progress will be hampered and stagnant.

As school leaders reflect upon their areas of improvement, consider using the following reflective questions in planning the action steps to advance your individual professional growth as well as the professional enhancement of your team.

In My Self-Evaluation and Assessment What leadership training, knowledge and best practices do I need to improve student learning?	How can I create a performance growth plan to serve as a roadmap for my professional learning and improvement?	How will I assess and track my progress and how will I know I have accomplished my professional learning goals?

I urge school leaders to make a commitment to become a better leader. I employ all school leaders to use this off-season time to stretch and to add value to their professional learning and growth. Student achievement is the "love thing" and it serves as the motivation and inspiration behind self-improvement and professional growth. Yes, champions are made in the off-season. Use this time wisely and strategically.

"Leadership is not about being in charge. It is about taking care of those in your charge."
—Simon Sinek

Chapter 11
New Principal's Message

When given the opportunity to speak before new principals, the message I prepared served as a summary of some of the lessons I learned along the way and have outlined within this book. May it encourage you to approach instructional leadership with heart, humility and with steadfast determination on your journey to transforming your school.

Good evening,

I would like to thank Dr. Lynnn Myers for inviting me to participate in this evening's activities and especially to be with newly appointed and first year principals. How honored I am to be with you tonight.

I can remember my first year as principal of Virginia Randolph Community High School, an alternative school in Henrico County. Dr. Mark Edwards, the superintendent, called me to his office and asked me to serve as principal at VRCHS. Now, I must admit and be honest and say that VRCHS was not on my radar or a part of my five-year plan. But it was the very best place for me to cut my principal teeth and learn.

As I sat at my desk for the first time behind the door marked Principal, I was suddenly struck with a feeling of terror: What in the heck have I gotten myself into? I no longer had the plate of an assistant principal. I now had the platter with all of the joys and responsibilities of the principal.

Leaders who step into new roles are always asking themselves three things:

1. *What do I need to do to preserve and honor the people before me?*

2. *What do I need to do in order to provide a sense of continuity of the past?*

3. *What do I need to change to send a clear signal that this is a new day and we are going in a new direction?*

Being the principal and leader of a school is a job filled with awesome responsibility, challenges and opportunities. Every day is different, spectacular, and involves high energy.

The challenges I don't have to tell you are unparalleled. Facing accountability for student achievement (NCLB, AYP, AMOs); implementing complex special education policies; Behavioral Intervention Plan (BIP), Functional Behavioral Assessment (FBA), IEP, ADHD, LRE (least restrictive environment), SSDI (social security disability insurance), ODD (Oppositional Defiant Disorder), RSP (Resource Specialist Plan) and RESPECT; providing for diverse student populations, being ever so mindful of safety issues and violence (Columbine HS, Sandy Hook); and dealing with parents who have been touched by angels: Heavenly Angels or Hell's Angels – just to name a few!

I am wearing my boots tonight as a reminder to me of the many piles of "dog poop" I stepped in over the years as principal. And if I lifted my shirt, you would see the battle scars received through many intense, yet growing situations.

Now, don't panic. I know you have plans after dinner. It has been a long day. I promise to give you the Elizabeth Taylor's version. Liz Taylor, the actress, had seven husbands. And she was clear to each when she announced to them: "Don't worry, darling! I'm not going to keep you long!"

This evening I have just four golden nuggets, or should I say McNuggets, for you to consider, ponder, massage. Four areas in focusing on your decisions in the years ahead: **Vision, Building Relationships, Teamwork,** and **Resolute Leadership**.

Vision is everything for a principal. It is utterly indispensable. Because vision leads the leader and the school. It paints the target. It conveys what you want the school to become.

It sparks and fuels the fire within and draws everyone forward. Show me a leader without vision, and I'll show you someone who isn't going anywhere.

Has anyone here ever put together a jigsaw puzzle? This helps you to understand what a vision is all about. Because on the top of the box is a complete picture of what the puzzle will look like once you get it together.

That's a vision of where you want things to end up. When you open the box, none of the pieces are together; none of the pieces are associated. And it takes time, energy, sweat, irritation, aggravation, motivation, frustration, dedication, elevation, and collaboration in order to put the pieces together.

But the vision on top of the box is what keeps you glued and keeps you focused and moving forward until the picture that is on top of the box becomes the vision that you have now put together.

And if you are ever going to put together the pieces of your school, you will need a picture of what it will look like when it is all said and done.

Find your vision, and let it guide you in all that you do.

And within that picture, it is important to communicate an image that will give your students and staff a reputation to uphold.

Give them something to aim for. It's putting something that was beyond their reach within their grasp. Why is it important? Because people will go farther than they thought they could when someone they respect tells them they can.

Years ago, a manager for the New York Yankees, Yogi Berra, wanted rookie players to know what a privilege it was to play for the team. He used to tell them, "Boys, it's an honor just to put on the New York Yankees pinstripes. So when you put them on, play like world champions. Play like Yankees. Play proud!"

Vision is everything. Take time to develop a high definition vision. You have to see it before you can be it.

Build Relationships

Building relationships is the foundation for a successful principalship.

Life in a school is hectic, but that's no excuse for not knowing the people you work with. Know their names.

Get out of the office. Let your people know who you are. Don't be stuck behind your title or desk, fly paper.

Share with your people what you believe in, and what you consider your "non-negotiables." Walk around the building often at different times of day. Visit classrooms and be present in the lunchroom, on the playground, and in the staff rooms.

As you move about campus, give your staff the "Triple A Treatment" (attention, affirmation and appreciation).

The next time you make contact with people, begin by giving them your undivided attention. Affirm them, their strengths, their value and show your appreciation for them early and often. Then watch what happens. Affirming someone is oxygen to the soul.

If you want to make others feel like a million bucks, learn to give your compliments in front of others as well as one-on-one.

Why? Because private compliments turned public, instantly and dramatically increase in value. Whenever you have the opportunity to publicly praise another person, don't let that moment slip by.

New Principal's Message

If you want to touch people and change lives, you have to touch them relationally first. Don't tell them what you know. You don't impress them with your knowledge; you impress them with your compassion.

A too common mistake principals make is failure to share recognition and show appreciation to others. The number one cause of dissatisfaction among staff was their administrators' failure to give them credit or their attempt to hog the spotlight.

Let me try to illustrate it. The story is told of a frog who lived in Canada. As winter arrived, he couldn't stand the cold, frigid weather.

He sat there one day watching the geese from Canada flying south and he shouted from the ground, "Can I fly with you?" And they responded, "You can't fly!" The frog feeling hopeful replied, "I know, but I found this piece of string and I thought if you put this string in your mouth and put a piece in his mouth, I can clamp on and fly down south with you for the winter."

They agreed and everything was going well. They were all flying together. Everything was great until they came over the farmlands of Goochland. A farmer was standing out in his field, and he looked up and saw those two birds flying with a piece of string in their mouths, and the frog clamped on in the middle.

He took off his hat and scratched his head and said, "My! My! My! Whoever thought of that must have been a genius." The frog heard him and just couldn't stand to let the glory pass, so he shouted, " I thought of it!" And down he went and the farmer had frog legs for dinner.

We would be amazed at what we could get done if we didn't care who got the credit.

The bottom line in building relationships isn't how far we advance ourselves, but how far we advance others.

Don't pursue glory; pursue excellence.

William H. Parker

Teamwork: We are Better Together!

The truth is that teamwork is at the heart of great achievement. The day I realized I could not do everything myself was a major step in my development as a person and as a leader.

I realized that when the vision gets bigger than you, you really only have two choices: give up on the vision or get help. I chose to get help and build a team. I needed staff buy-in and others to have skin in the game.

I realized that when the challenges escalate, teamwork must elevate! And as John Maxwell says, *"Teamwork Makes the Dream Work!"*

The story is told of a man's request for disability which was denied pending clarification of that request. The insurance company wrote to him because the basis of his claim was not clear.

Here is what he wrote back: To whom it may concern, I am writing a response to your request for additional information in block #3 of the accident report form. I wrote "trying to do the job alone" as the cause of my accident.

You said in your letter to me that I should more fully explain, and I trust that the following details will be sufficient. I am a bricklayer by trade. On the day of the accident I was working alone on the roof of a six-story building.

When I completed my work, I discovered that I had approximately 500 pounds of brick left over. Not wanting to waste it, and rather than carry the bricks down by hand, I decided to lower them in a barrel by using the pulley that was attached to the side of the building at the sixth floor.

Securing the rope at ground level, I went up to the roof. I swung the barrel out and then loaded the bricks into it. I then went down to the ground and untied the rope holding it tightly to ensure a slow descent of the brick.

New Principal's Message

You will note in block #2 of the accident report, it says that I weigh 135 pounds. Due to my surprise, and being jerked off the ground, I lost my presence of mind and did not let go of the rope.

Needless to say, I proceeded at a rather rapid rate up the side of the building. In the vicinity of the third floor, I met the barrel coming down. This explains my broken collar bone. Slowed only slightly, I continued my rapid ascent up the side of the building until the fingers of my right hand were two knuckles deep in the pulley six floors up.

Fortunately, I had the presence of mind to hold on to the rope in spite of my pain. At approximately the same time, however, the barrel hit the ground, the bottom came off, the bricks spilled out and without the weight of the bricks, the barrel only weighs fifty pounds and I weigh according to block #2, 135 pounds.

Therefore, as you might imagine, I began a rapid descent down the side of the building, and in the vicinity of the third floor, I again met the barrel coming back up. This accounts for my fractured ankles and the lacerations on my lower body.

The encounter with the barrel slowed me down enough to lessen my injuries when I landed on top of the pile of bricks. I was lying there in pain and the pain was so intense I was unable to move, and thinking about my pain, I let go of the rope.

Because my eyes were closed, I did not see the barrel coming back down until it broke both of my legs. I hope I have furnished enough information to explain how the accident occurred. It occurred because I was trying to do the job alone.

I challenge you to think of one act of genuine significance in the history of humankind that was performed by a lone human being. No matter what you name, you will find that a team of people was involved. Remember, one is too small a number to achieve greatness.

If you want something big, you must link up with others. Why take the journey alone when you can invite others along with you? Because we are better together!

Leadership (Resolute Leadership)

"The ultimate measure of a man is not where he stands in moments of comfort, but where he stands at times of challenge and controversy." – MLK

Resolute Leadership (Courage) is absolutely necessary in transforming a school. You must have the tenacity to reach your capacity, determination, and backbone in holding the line on behaviors that may be in conflict with the school's mission and values.

As principal, you must decide whether you want to be popular or effective.

In my first year as principal of Henrico High School, our administrative team non-renewed eight teachers. These teachers did not represent the professional nor instructional qualities required to continue wearing the "Green and Gold." They did not pass the "litmus test."

Question: Would you want your child in their classroom?

Believe me, it would have been much easier to look the other way or use the rationale, "I don't want to hurt their feelings." Really, it was my feelings that I wanted to protect.

After months of intervention, support, guidance and direction, we decided to move forward with dismissal. Time was of the essence! Student success was the motivating factor. We lovingly nurtured them to grow or go!

This reminds me of a superintendent of a big city school district. One day he met with one of his principals to ask why the children in his school were consistently underperforming.

New Principal's Message

The principal took the superintendent to the window in his office, pointed to the children entering the school, and said, "You see those poor kids? Most of them have one parent, if that. They can't read and they probably don't even speak the language. They just aren't going to make it! The superintendent, after hearing an earful of excuses and alibis, fired the principal that day. True story!

Wow! What a decision! What a message! Yet, each of you has to answer the same question. How will you and your school respond when students struggle and have difficulty learning? How will you organize your school to increase student achievement in all of your student groups?

This is the million dollar question of every school.

The reality is if you are not winning with your students, you badly need to re-examine your beliefs, your behavior, your message, your language and rethink your strategies and tactics.

This superintendent took action and demonstrated that this principal's "stinking thinking" and poor response were unacceptable.

This was a defining moment in this district. And there is a defining moment for you and your school as well.

What will you do when students in your building are struggling and having difficulty? It will not take long for your community to see!

If you ignore a situation that is not in alignment with your school's mission and values, you just sent out a clear message. Your silence just endorsed the negative behavior.

Principals, you are the quality control persons of your school and "Standard Bearer." You set the tone and expectations.

It takes courage and resolute leadership to be the "guardian of the process" of the school. What you do or don't do will convey what is important to you.

Your responsibility is always to put students first and to make clear that there is only one agenda for every classroom in your school. That agenda must be driven by the single belief that we serve all of our students really well, regardless of their differences.

Every Child, Every Day! Not Some of the Children, Some of the Time!

Dr. Myers, can we take it a step further? Principals, do you have the courage to drill deeper into your school's data to uncover and erase systemic inequities in your school?

Is there equity in your talented and gifted program? Your advanced placement courses? Does your staff represent the demographics of your school?

Is there an over-identification of African-American and Hispanics students in Special Education?

Is there more than a 10% achievement gap among your white, black, Hispanic and poor students? If so, the question for you is, what course of action will you take to create new patterns of equity, fairness and support in your school?

Are their gatekeepers upholding the status quo or are you "widening the net" to include underrepresented students who are full of ability, motivated and willing to work hard?

Does your staff believe that external causes are sufficient reasons to not educate all children well?

Or have they switched from deficit thinking to an asset orientation in their thinking about children?

Does your staff focus on what students don't have or do they focus instead on what assets, gifts, strengths, and abilities they do have and how we might build on those assets so that all students can be successful?

New Principal's Message

Please know the success of our society is directly dependent on our ability as educators to be successful with children of color, with whom we have not been very successful with in the past.

Until we passionately believe and vigorously behave in excellence and equity, it is hard to imagine that we will ever convince anyone else to believe or behave.

And if you wouldn't follow you, why should anyone else?

If you don't have the ability to see when to stand up and have the conviction to do it, you'll never be an effective leader. When a brave man takes a stand, the spines of others are stiffened. A show of courage by a leader will encourage others.

Well, I hope this after dinner appetizer of McNuggets has given you something to think about as you prepare and plan for the upcoming school year.

Know that the first year as principal is the toughest. No other point is the responsibility leap and learning curve as large.

As you go forward this year, keep in mind the importance of vision and let it guide you in all that you do. Remember you have to see it in order to be it.

Take time to build relationships as it is the foundation for a successful principalship. Remember, if you get along, they'll go along.

Take time to develop and strengthen teamwork in your building because one is too small a number to achieve greatness. Individuals play the game, but teams win championships.

Become a resolute leader. Stay on message and have the courage to do what is right for all children in your building, especially the "least of these." Remember one person with courage is a majority.

Believe me, it gets better and easier as you gain your stripes. Remember, you don't get medals without the wounds.

You don't have a testimony until you go through a test. You don't have a message until you go through some mess.

And don't forget to wear your boots. I guarantee that there will be some "dog poop" somewhere along your journey. Just keep stepping forward!

Thank you!

When I reflect upon my years of instructional service and leadership, I am extremely grateful to have had the opportunity to serve and work with so many outstanding educators and leaders who supported, encouraged and lifted me. They were excellent examples of how love and exhibiting a high regard for students and staff would transform lives and schools. Throughout my career as a teacher, department chair, assistant principal, principal, central office executive and principal coach, I have observed and experienced how vital and powerful love, compassion and deeply valuing your students and team can have a tremendous impact on the success of a school.

Instructional leadership is about caring passionately, intently and vigorously enough to create positive change and make the courageous choices needed in the school community to escalate achievement. Everybody in the school needs a champion — staff members included! I urge you to place your students and staff ahead of yourself to build a strong sense of connectedness and community. Kindness is the most powerful, least costly, and most underrated agent of human change. On any given day, there will be a call to duty to stand in the gap and be that advocate and supporter that some student or staff member needs.

So school leaders, I employ you to amplify your love and compassion for your school community. Allow love for your students and team to be at the core of every school decision. Let it be evident and visible in your school values; in your vision, culture, professional training, school and instructional planning; instructional delivery; extra help opportunities; use of data; teacher evaluations;

New Principal's Message

selection of students for your most rigorous courses, and more. Let love lead you in caring enough to hold the line on behaviors that are contrary to the school's mission and values. Love and commitment are the forces that stand you up in the morning with conviction and duty to ensure you are meeting the needs of every child, every day.

Remember, love is an action verb and its power is profound in transforming mediocrity and average into excellence. Kindness and love are the things school leaders need most in touching and transforming lives. Be reminded, leading with heart is a love thing and is an essential component in transforming and elevating schools to exceptional levels of service and achievement. Lead with Love!

After all, leading with heart is a love thing.

Works Cited

Bell, Brené. *The Gifts of Imperfection: Let Go of Who You Think You're Supposed to Be and Embrace Who You Are.* Hazelden Publishing, 2010.

Brown, Brené. *Daring Greatly: How the Courage to Be Vulnerable Transforms the Way We Live, Love, Parent, and Lead.* Gotham Books, 2012.

Collins, Jim. *Good to Great: Why Some Companies Make the Leap...and Others Don't.* HarperBusiness, 2001.

Crenshaw, Kimberlé. "Mapping the Margins: Intersectionality, Identity Politics, and Violence against Women of Color." *Stanford Law Review*, vol. 43, no. 6, 1991, pp. 1241–1299.

Deming, W. Edwards. *Out of the Crisis.* MIT Center for Advanced Engineering Study, 1986.

hooks, bell. *All About Love: New Visions.* William Morrow, 2000.

Jones, Fredric H. *Tools for Teaching: Discipline, Instruction, Motivation.* Fredric H. Jones & Associates, Inc., 2000.

Lewis, C. S. *The Four Loves.* Harcourt Brace, 1960.

Maxwell, John. *The 21 Irrefutable Laws of Leadership: Follow Them and People Will Follow You.* Thomas Nelson, 2007.

Neff, Kristin. *Self-Compassion: The Proven Power of Being Kind to Yourself*. William Morrow, 2011.

Pankake, Anita, and Jesus (Chuey) Abrego, Jr. *Lead with Me: A Principal's Guide to Teacher Leadership*. 2nd ed., Routledge, 2017.

Park, Todd. "Data by Itself Is Useless." *TEDMED*, 2012, www.tedmed.com.

"Ownership of Learning." *Edutopia*, George Lucas Educational Foundation, 5 Oct. 2016, www.edutopia.org/discussion/ownership-learning.

Rice, Jennifer King. *Teacher Quality: Understanding the Effectiveness of Teacher Attributes*. Economic Policy Institute, 2003.

Scheurich, James Joseph, and Linda Skrla. *Leadership for Equity and Excellence: Creating High-Achievement Classrooms, Schools, and Districts*. Corwin Press, 2003.

Tutu, Desmond, and Mpho Tutu. *The Book of Forgiving: The Fourfold Path for Healing Ourselves and Our World*. HarperOne, 2014.

Weiner, Jeff. "Data Really Powers Everything That We Do." *LinkedIn*, LinkedIn Corporation, www.linkedin.com/pulse/data-really-powers-everything-we-do-jeff-weiner.

West, Cornel. *Race Matters*. Beacon Press, 1993.

William H. Parker, affectionately known as Bill, is a veteran educator and transformational school leader with more than four decades of experience in teaching, administration, and leadership coaching. A graduate of Virginia Union University (B.A., Elementary Education, 1975) and Virginia Commonwealth University (M.Ed., Administration and Supervision, 1984), Parker began his career as a social studies teacher at Henderson Middle School, where he taught for ten years before moving into school leadership.

He went on to serve as assistant principal at Henderson Middle, Henrico High, and Highland Springs High Schools, and later as principal of Virginia Randolph Community High School and Henrico High School. Under his leadership, Henrico High achieved full accreditation in his first year as principal. Parker's innovative leadership earned him multiple honors, including **Henrico County Public Schools Instructional Leader of the Year (2003)**, **Richmond Area Black School Administrator Instructional Leader of the Year (2003)**, **Community Foundation R.E.B. Instructional Leader of the Year (2006)**, and **Virginia High School Principal of the Year (2007)**.

Beyond his principalships, Parker has contributed to education as an adjunct professor at Virginia Commonwealth University, a workshop presenter at the Virginia Superintendents' Conference, and a consultant supporting schools in Richmond and across Virginia. After retiring from the Virginia public school system in 2007, he continued to shape education as a **Principal Coach** and **Executive Director of Secondary Education and Career and Technical Education in Mooresville, NC**, and later as **Vice President of Community Development for ChallengeU**, a dropout recovery program. His leadership in Mooresville helped propel the district to the #2 academic ranking in North Carolina and raise the African American graduation rate from 60% to 95%.

Throughout his career, Parker has worked with state departments of education, public school districts, and national consulting firms, providing coaching, leadership development, and turnaround strategies for struggling schools. His work has impacted communities across Virginia, North Carolina, and Indiana, leaving a legacy of excellence, equity, and student-centered leadership.

www.ingramcontent.com/pod-product-compliance
Lightning Source LLC
Chambersburg PA
CBHW050639160426
43194CB00010B/1729